Cedar County

Cedar County

A Memoir of Iowa

Steve Sanger

Writers Club Press
New York Lincoln Shanghai

Cedar County
A Memoir of Iowa

Writers Club Press
an imprint of iUniverse, Inc.

For information address:
iUniverse, Inc.
2021 Pine Lake Road, Suite 100
Lincoln, NE 68512
www.iuniverse.com

Front cover photo: Courtesy of author, taken in 1944 on Will Sanger farm west of Wapello, Iowa. Author's father, Lysle Sanger, is at the wheel with author's brother Duane and cousin Diane on his lap. Author's grandfather, Will, standing behind. Author is at far right. Others in photo are cousins of author.

ISBN: 0-595-26508-1

Printed in the United States of America

Contents

1

On a morning in the late winter of 1945, I walked along a gravel road to the one-room country school north of our tenant farm in Cedar County, Iowa, and wondered what I would do if Adolf Hitler came along and offered me a ride. I was in the third grade and had read enough about the war to know Hitler was in trouble. My recollection is that if the Fuehrer had driven up and asked me if I wanted a lift, I would have said, "No, thanks."

That time was good for me. After the shades of gray and brown and stark white of winter, the scene would soon be changing to the green of corn and alfalfa and timothy hay and soy beans, and a brushing of yellow as the oats ripened. I was almost nine years old. Cedar County was idyllic. I remember good times, the heavy fresh smell of new-turned soil, the sweetness of new-mown hay. I remembered well those green and golden fields, a sense of worthwhile work, close family life, neighborliness, recollections of secure benevolence spiced by wartime drama. Franklin Roosevelt died that April, and I couldn't wait to tell my dad the news when he came in from the field. I jumped on the Farmall's drawbar and shouted above the engine noise, "FDR's dead."

The war in Europe ended in May and my grandpa Albert Ratzlaff stood in the barnyard and gave me a nickel to celebrate the survival of my uncle, Daryl, his only son, my mother's brother, a combat medic in General Patton's army. The next big event of '45 was the surrender of Japan and the end of the war. We drove into Iowa City that night in August and the church bells were ringing and the central downtown streets were jammed with happy people. I don't suppose that has happened since, except for student riots or maybe if Iowa beat Michigan in football.

In the winter at the Prairie Bell school the favorite game was "fox and geese" in the snow. Some of the students rode ponies to school and the Martins, two sisters and a brother, often came in a pony cart. It must have been a prosperous time too because of the wartime economy.

Saturday evenings, right after chores, we drove north 10 miles on chuck-holed blacktop to Tipton, the county seat. I always had a chocolate malt at Zager's Drug, prepared by Olon, the druggist, a high school buddy of my dad. We went to shows at the Hardacre Theater, usually a western or a war movie. Tipton was dominated then by a tall Victorian courthouse with a clock tower. In my memory the clock is stuck at a little before 7 p.m., time enough to have a malt and make the first show. On Saturday nights during the summer, farmers sat on the fenders or running boards of their cars angle-parked on courthouse square and talked while their wives shopped.

◆   ◆   ◆

In 1988, influenced by these memories as well as a growing dislike for my job as a newspaper reporter in Seattle and an almost total lack of financial or social obligations, I asked for my last pay check and went back to Cedar County. The idea was to observe life, get into the rhythm of a country town and write about it in a low-key reportorial manner. I was born in Iowa City, went to City High and the university there, and sometimes when life was lonely or fragmented I yearned to go home, at least for a little while. Cedar County, a place of pleasant childhood memories, seemed a smart choice, rather than Iowa City. I wanted a rural place that hadn't changed too much. A place where I could get a handle on life, some place that was manageable, and where I could more easily afford the cost of living. I wanted to go back to a place that reminded me of growing up in the country. I had no romantic notion of the beauties of rural living. I had been the son of a tenant farmer too long.

In addition, my family had a history in Cedar County, even though no Sangers lived in the county anymore and hadn't since my family lived on the tenant farm for a year in '45. Something else I found oddly appealing about Tipton and Cedar County. Symmetry. Cedar County is 24 miles square, and right smack-dab in the middle like a bulls-eye the pioneers built Tipton.

◆   ◆   ◆

My second ex-wife told me, more than once, that all my moving around, which had been considerable—Iowa, Ohio, California, Hawaii, England, the Pacific Northwest—was only a sign I was trying to finish my dad's life for him. She was on to something. My old man had followed a gloriously itinerant life in the early 1930s, jobless years of the Great Depression, traveling through the West, often on freight trains, following the harvests or impulse. The Dakotas, Montana, New Mexico and Southern California, living off the land, once going to jail in Needles, California, for stealing gas out of a road grader. As happens, my dad got married and settled down in Iowa. He never lost his restlessness, and talked a lot about a little spread in the West, a few cows and freedom. My dad settled for taking my brother and me to western movies. Later, I realized he had a lot of the Willy Loman kind of dreaming in him, and I inherited a lot of it, or absorbed it as a boy. I typified what some refer to as "the Rand McNally approach to self-discovery." Closer, maybe, to something Kerouac wrote: "Traveled a lot of miles, never got anywhere."

◆   ◆   ◆

In addition to these personal romances, my dad's side of the family had deep roots in Cedar County. Three generations of Sangers had been farmers in the county. That sense of place carried weight with me, since I was an un-propertied drifter, a grease monkey in the service station of American journalism. The Cedar County portion of the history of my dad's family went back to the mid-1850s, when my dad's grandfather, John Sanger, and John's older brother, George, left England, with a couple of trunks and their flint lock muskets, and sailed for America on a four-masted schooner.

That version of the story came from my grandfather, Will. But he was only 14 years old when his father, John, died and thus may not have got the story quite straight. Another version, likely more accurate, came from Will's cousin, Jelena, daughter of George. In 1939, she told my dad's younger brother, Lester, the family historian, that her father and his twin brother, William, left England's Suffolk County in the early 1850s following a family setback. George went to America, and William sailed to Australia, the idea being to check out the two countries, compare notes and then settle in the more congenial place. William was never heard from again, and no one ever knew why. I tried to find out years ago how many Sangers there were in Australia. Lots of them, it turned out, but I never found out if they were related to the long-lost William. I wrote one of the Sangers listed in the Melbourne telephone book. He, to my family's surprise, was a rabbi who had fled Hitler and settled in Austrialia. At that point, I abandoned the search.

But, back to the 1850s. After the long silence from William, George wrote John, then in his early 20s, and asked him to meet him in New York City.

The reason the three brothers decided to leave England was simple. Their father, also named William, had inherited a game preserve in East Suffolk, near Wickham Market, and was considered reasonably well-to-do. In about 1838, after his wife's death, William went to the Continent, and gambled away whatever fortune he had. This setback apparently so discouraged his three sons that they decided to leave home.

◆   ◆   ◆

One summer afternoon, not long ago, I took a walk in the country not far from Wickham Market in East Suffolk where my dad's paternal ancestors came from. The rural landscape was not much different from Cedar County. Slightly rolling, very green, extensively cultivated. The crops were different. Wheat, a little corn, barley, sugar beets, oilseed, potatoes, vegetables. Sheep and dairy cows. Population was denser and usually a village with its church spire was in view. Ancient country too, as far as human habitation was concerned. People lived in Suffolk hundreds of years before the Roman invasion in the First Century A.D. Even so, one 21st Century aspect was the same as Cedar County. You could smell pigs in the wind.

◆   ◆   ◆

At any rate, John did meet George in New York City and before long they had left there to work at an upstate dairy farm, then a coal mine and in a year or so wound up in Iowa City. From Iowa City, they traveled 15 miles east to Springdale, in western Cedar County, to become, first, hired farm hands, then entrepreneurs. They bought oxen and a plow and broke virgin sod for other settlers. Eventually, in a few years, after cutting wood in the winter and operating a limestone pit, they purchased brush land from squatters between Springdale and Cedar Valley. The bachelor brothers lived together in a two-room shanty. In 1858 George sold the 40 acres to George and bought land and a house in Gower Township two miles northeast.

John stayed in the shanty for several more years. By 1859 both bachelors were married to young women who had come into Cedar County as pioneers from Ohio and Michigan. In August, 1862, before the crops were harvested, the restless brothers traveled to Muscatine, Iowa, enlisted for three years in the Grand Army of the Republic and went south for the duration. George was 31; John was 29, with one child and another on the way. The family history doesn't detail how their wives coped with the farm work during their husbands' absence.

While browsing in the Tipton Public Library, I came across a record of their enlistment in Company G of the 35th Regiment, Iowa Volunteer Infantry. They fought unscathed at Vicksburg, Tupelo, Nashville, and in one of the Civil War's last fights, at Mobile Bay. Mustered out in August, 1865, still in Co. G, they were home in time for a Cedar County autumn.

Few details of their Civil War experiences survive. All letters were lost and neither man talked much about the war. When they came home, the brothers brought a liberated slave with them, a youth named George Tyler, who worked on the brothers' farms for several years. Little more was recorded about Tyler whose story must have been the stuff of legend.

Two other legends, temporarily, were part of the Sanger story. In early versions, oral and written, of my Uncle Lester's family histories, Sidney and Beatrice Webb, inventors of British socialism, and Jesse and Frank James, if not the inventors, at least innovators, of the train robbery, were mentioned as shirttail relatives. Being related to the James' boys excited me as a boy, and there were heart-pounding stories of Jesse and Frank, on the run, resting their horses late at night at Cedar County farms, aided by my grandmother's relatives. In his later definitive account, Uncle Lester deleted the Webbs and the James boys, for lack of evidence.

Another memory was that a portion of the little Friends Cemetery north of Springdale, surrounded by farmland, was sprinkled with my family name. A mile or two east of the Friends Cemetery is another country burying ground, called North Liberty, and here some of my dad's maternal ancestors, the Bates, were buried.

My grandfather, Will Sanger, born in 1871, remembered going by wagon with his parents and five brothers and sisters to Iowa City for the celebration of America's first 100 years. A very hot day, he remembered, and they had to rest the horses many times during the 15-mile trip. Will died in Iowa City at the age of 93 in 1965. He was a great talker, storyteller and reader. He seemed old all my life, although always vigorous and somewhat domineering. A favorite story was how he cast his first presidential vote in 1896 for William McKinley and never again voted for a Republican. He admired Franklin Roosevelt, partly because of FDR's farm programs during the Depression. Will also admired Winston Churchill and when he went to the hospital in Iowa City where he died, my grandfather took along a couple of books by Churchill.

In 1900 Will bought 83 acres northeast of Springdale. The little farm included an old house which stood abandoned for many years and was demolished while I lived in Tipton. He soon tired of his own cooking and moved next door to live with the H.K. Maxson family which included three sons and Nellie Bates, who was Mrs. Maxson's daughter from her first marriage to the late George F. Bates. Two years later Will married Nellie, a school teacher. Nellie's mother, Anna Maxson, was a Phelps, another old and distinguished name in Cedar County.

Soon after their marriage they moved to Rodman, in northwestern Iowa, where Will and his brother George had bought a farm. Will and Nellie moved around a lot after that, mostly farming, always in Iowa, and had nine children, eight surviving into adulthood. Their children always called them "Papa" and "Mama."

A couple of times while I was living in Tipton, Uncle Lester came from his home in Lincoln, Nebraska, and we drove slowly on the back roads in the Springdale area. Lester, who had total recall, showed me where our relatives had lived. One favorite spot was a grassy corner of a field on the road between Springdale and Cedar Valley. This empty corner was where the shanty had stood, the one where John and George had lived in the 1850s and where Will Sanger was born in 1871.

Inexplicably, and it was a sore subject with me, in spite of being on the scene early and owning a good deal of land, none of this Cedar County real estate stayed in the family. Not a Sanger remained in Cedar County, until I went back for my sojourn. I didn't exactly belong there but I was not quite a stranger.

◆   ◆   ◆

Sitting at my desk, a 51-year-old reporter at the *Seattle Post-Intelligencer*, groggy in mind and spirit, I found this Cedar County musing to be heady stuff. When I reached a magical figure in my credit union account, and after I convinced myself that the greatest risk is the avoidance of all risk, well, I decided to go, remembering William Least Heat Moon's motto in *Blue Highways*: "If you can't make a go of your life, you can at least go."

I figured I wasn't making much of a go. Two divorces. Futile, sometimes disappointing, sometimes demeaning escapades with women. Romances gone the way of the buffalo and the dodo bird. "Dead as the Whigs," as my dad's dad used to say when he wanted to express finality. An occasional love affair leaving icicles in my heart and gut. A job I found wanting. I was a man burdened with gloomy attitudes and vague longings. "Estranged, alone and medium gray."

My escape from routine banality was to head over the Cascades with my old '94 Winchester saddle gun and walk and do some informal target shooting along the east side of the Columbia River a few miles north of Vantage. This area is a low-rent Monument Valley, which fit in nicely with my favorite western movie fantasies, leftovers from Saturday nights at the Hardacre in Tipton.

Like the Jack Nicholson character in the movie *Five Easy Pieces*, I had moved around a lot, not because I was looking for something but "to get away from things that go bad if I stay." An ear for auspicious beginnings. With some uneasiness, I remembered Clifford Odets, who wrote near the end of his life about "that miserable patch of events, that melange of nothing, while you were looking for something to happen, that was it! That was life! You lived it!" I figured it was time to stop running lateral plays along the line of scrimmage. One fear was to wake up in a nursing home, disabled in some hopeless way, and asking myself why I hadn't taken chances when I was able, before action became an abstraction.

A barely-controlled bad attitude about one's daily work is common among newspaper reporters too long in the same harness. I was part of that tradition, in spades. I got along poorly with most of the editors, and considered few were qualified to carry my jock strap. To me, editors, as a group, were all hat and no cattle.

As a rule, male reporters I knew castrated themselves one way or another, with no help from editors. Mortgages and financial obligations in general, surrendering to materialism and the demands of aggressively expensive wives and kids. They were wage slaves. A Mafia wiseguy, who had contempt for the working stiff, put it into perspective. He said these sorts of people were "pension-plan creatures, neutered by compliance and awaiting their turn to die."

Eventually, the relationship between editor and reporter may become a matter of authority first, and all else, including intelligence, were down the line. No mutual respect, threats instead. When that happened to me, it was time to saddle up. I was blessed because I had no mortgage or expensive wife or dependent children to hog-tie me.

I had some pretty fair innings over the years. I had worked mostly as a reporter but with erratic periods as a desk editor and spent two years writing editorials in Honolulu. My newspaper life began in 1959 as a copy boy in San Francisco at the *News-Call Bulletin*, which died in the 1960s. Then, journalism graduate school in Iowa City until I got sick of the abstract nature of the academic life and decided to abandon graduate courses and write for the student paper, the *Daily Iowan*. I went on to Springfield, Ohio; The Associated Press in Fresno and San Francisco; both dailies in Honolulu, followed by the *Fresno Bee*. My last paper and where I stayed the longest was the *Post-Intelligencer*, the Hearst morning daily in Seattle.

Nice datelines. Berlin, Brussels, Seoul, Belfast, Papeete, Chicago, New York. A memorable train ride between Anchorage and Fairbanks, another one between Frankfurt and Berlin. Marching down Broadway with the Vietnam vets, a jail cell interview with a 16-year-old murderer, conversations with prime ministers, daughters of presidents and Supreme Court justices. I covered legislatures and exciting trials, stories about nuclear weapons, riots, floods, airplane crashes, train wrecks. Deadline pressure, swinging for the fences, home runs. I rode in a B-17, spent a couple of hours with a man who survived the Nagasaki raid. My favorite story of all, though, out of the hundreds I wrote, was a low-key account of the winter wheat harvest on a family-farm operation in eastern Washington.

◆   ◆   ◆

During the summer of 1986, I took a six-month leave to do research coast-to-coast for an oral history of Hanford, the Manhattan Project operation in southeastern Washington state that manufactured the plutonium used in the first atomic bomb explosion at Trinity Site in New Mexico, and for the bomb which destroyed Nagasaki. When I asked for more time off, without pay, to write the book, the newspaper management refused. An associate, documentary film-maker Bob Mull, and I wrote it during the winter, and by the time I had quit the paper, the manuscript was being considered for publication by a university press. While in Tipton, this publisher rejected it, which caused considerable consternation and gnashing of teeth. Eventually, after rewriting and revision, it was submitted to other publishers and during my Tipton stay the manuscript's fate was in doubt.

(Eventually I published the book myself in 1989 and after this edition sold out, Portland State University re-published an expanded edition titled *Working on the Bomb*.)

After a summer of talking to Manhattan Project veterans, including some eminent physicists who knew Einstein, my mind was elsewhere when I returned to the paper. I was assigned to what seemed like an increasingly insulting round of near-trivia. During my last year at the newspaper, I talked to bus drivers of the year, wrote about pets of the month, did daily stories for weeks about an eccentric Vietnam vet who was trying to starve himself to death, interviewed Christmas shoppers at shopping centers, covered the Rotary Club, and once was told, in October, to check major shopping areas to see if anyone had put up Christmas decorations. A telephone interview with Rudolf Hess's dentist, by contrast with my usual stuff, was a plum assignment. I did a long project about Seattle's peace movement which had taken literally years to set up and accomplish. An editor was quoted as saying he didn't like the piece because "it had too much information."

Like most reporters, I had started by covering small stories, an occasional traffic fatality, police court, harmless interviews with harmless people. I went on to legislatures and presidents and foreign datelines, but by 1987 was working my way back to injury accidents and fatals, Rotary Club speeches by podiatrists, and how to dispose of lawn cuttings. My schedule became 3 p.m. to midnight, including Sundays, a shift my buddy the city editor called "the slag heap." During my performance evaluation, I was described as a competent writer and reporter, an experienced man with a bad attitude who didn't try to hide his contempt for the business or his superiors. More interested in the big picture than local events, basically antagonistic, uncooperative and argumentative. Fair description, I thought. I was slightly annoyed but not surprised when my pay raise was something like $3 a week because I "sometimes failed to meet standards." I began to have a feeling of joy and well being when I woke up on my days off. My dream scenario was to have someone ask me at a party, "What do you do?" and to reply, "I used to be a newspaper reporter."

I could hear the beat, but I refused to dance to it anymore. I quit the paper after almost 14 years, and nobody but my peers and one supervisor said goodbye when I left the city room. A fellow sufferer on 3-12 sent me an electronic message: "Walk with the wind." If I hadn't resigned when I did I could easily have wound up in a loony-bin or prison. My mental status was that volatile. In spite of giving up a comfortable salary and cushy Newspaper Guild benefits, I have never regretted the decision.

My last night, I wrote my advance obituary and filed it with the newspaper morgue. I decided to add an epitaph and chose 2 Timothy 4:7: "I have fought a good fight. I have finished my course. I have kept the faith."

◆   ◆   ◆

It was time to slap leather. My mount, a little long in the tooth, was an autumnal '77 VW Rabbit, a veteran of 200,000 miles, most of them highway. When I left that last day of January and turned south on Interstate 5, I had $17,000 in the credit union, $55,000 worth of New York Stock Exchange common stocks (mostly electric utilities), $10,000 in mutual funds, $300 in my pocket, some odds and ends of money in other accounts, bringing the total to $82,400, depending on the state of the stock market at any given moment. I owed $400 to the IRS.

I gave away my furniture, stored some paintings, books, and mementoes and my Winchester Model '94. Otherwise, everything I owned went with me, including my faded red Raleigh Super Course on the VW's bicycle rack, my Kaypro computer and Juki printer riding on the passenger seat, belted in. Frustration dogged me at my first overnight. I stopped at a former girlfriend's place, and thought maybe I could sleep with her again, for luck, for the road. Her response was, "Sleep on the couch. You're leaving the state, and I may never see you again. What's the use?"

My only satisfaction was that she almost cried when I left early the next morning. On the car radio, I heard a weather report that said I-5 over Siskiyou Pass into California was snow-packed and chains would be required. I didn't care. On the way south, my mind wandered considerably, but stubbornly returned to the frame of mind described in my journal the night before I left Seattle.

"The hard time has come. Until tonight I have felt good about what I am doing. Scared, anxious, and confident. Tonight, I am feeling very alone and a little idiotic. A touch of hysteria. The apartment is almost empty. I am lonely. I see snapshots of snowy Iowa City inside my head. The farewells are flattering, but exhausting. My nerve is slipping. Have I lost my mind? Probably."

I reminded myself of a couple of things. My decision to change direction was inspired by several events, besides occupational sickness. A brother had gone to prison, a friend was raped, two close friends had incurable diseases, all of which lent credence to the old saying, "We are not guaranteed tomorrow."

In fact, I had left a lot behind in Seattle. Wonderful and delightful friends, ex-lovers and ex-wives I was very fond of, my daughter Nellie, who was studying art and French literature at the University of Washington. I left behind a life, one that was used up, but it was familiar and had had its moments. When I gave away my possessions, a reporter friend said I was doing what people did before they killed themselves. I told him, "Yeah, in a way that's right, except I am not killing myself, I am killing a way of life that deserves it." People told me they admired my guts in quitting a $38,000 a year job and heading into apparent oblivion. I always answered it wasn't bravery, it was necessity. I was like a guy swimming with sharks; I had to get out of the water or be eaten. I had to save myself. It was the road un-taken or the nuthouse. The most reassuring comment came from an ex-girl friend, who came over to say goodbye, started to cry and managed to blubber, before she fled, "You are doing the right thing."

◆   ◆   ◆

I stopped in Portland to see my buddy Dick Hoyt, a successful novelist and friend from the 1960s when we were reporters together in Honolulu. Dr. Dick the Dick Doctor and I had traveled a lot of miles together, including one trip around the world during which we rode the Trans-Siberian Express from east to west, described by Dick in one of his fairly rare poetic moments, as "riding from winter into spring." I was obviously a little down in the mouth and he said, "Feels like you been wrenched away from your roots, doesn't it? Really lonely."

We talked about his novel in progress. He called it a masterpiece. Dr. Dick fixed a bachelor's cheap lunch of wieners from Fred Meyer, yellow mustard, cole slaw in a plastic container and expensive ale from a micro-brewery in Mount Hood, Oregon. I was on my way in a couple of hours and made Yreka, California, before I slept at a Motel 6. Not a trace of snow on Siskiyou Pass.

◆   ◆   ◆

Coming into California on I-5 was always a sweet time for me. You had the downhill run off Siskiyou Summit, and after the "Welcome to California" sign, and if the day was clear or the night was moonlighted, magnificent glistening Mount Shasta filled the windshield. I liked California, was thrilled by it, had a soft spot. San Francisco was where I went when I left Iowa in '59. A place of journalistic wins, a marriage, children, San Francisco pleasures.

At Sacramento I left I-5 for California 99, the eucalyptus and oleander route through the San Joaquin Valley to Fresno where my younger brother Duane lived. We had a few Rainier ales (the Green Death) and I relaxed before the big push east. I had lived in Fresno years before, back in the days when you could smell the orange blossoms over the ozone and could see the Sierra most days in the summer. I still enjoyed the town, and there was no more relaxed and generous host than my brother.

Relaxed atmosphere or not, I experienced moments of serious semi-panic. The kind of feeling that causes you to sit hunched, clasping your hands between your knees, eyes closed, teeth clenched, asking yourself, "What next?" Sleepless nights and despondent mornings with fears of old age, thoughts of loneliness, rootlessness, a lack of warmth, going home to aged parents, a long cold solitary ride east across the mountains and wintry high plains, headed away from the Land O'Dreams. This low mood persisted as I flogged the Rabbit across the Sierra, until near Lovelock, Nevada, a great big white-orange full moon blazed into sight. I convinced myself the dramatic event was a favorable omen.

Be strong, I told myself. Be resolute. Do the Cedar County project, worry about the future later. Look at this new beginning as an adventure, be a saddle tramp for a while. I could afford it, and certainly needed the change. This courage came from sitting at the bar in a Stateline, Nevada, casino drinking Coors and watching the weekday gamblers who came by chartered bus from Salt Lake. This interior pep talk was fine, but I had something to do over the line in Utah that couldn't be glossed over. I had to visit my youngest brother Bill at Utah State Prison.

◆   ◆   ◆

USP was south of Salt Lake, off I-15 on a little plain, with high snowy mountains around it. The visiting area was a cafeteria, with some men and women sitting as close as the rules allowed, playing cards, talking, sometimes laughing. Mothers sat near their sons, occasionally reaching across the table to hold hands. My brother and I drank a lot of coffee and hot chocolate out of the plastic glasses. We had a long talk. Bill was 15 years younger than me, an age difference so great we never got to know each other well before I moved away.

He was lean, almost ascetic, wearing clean pressed prison blues, his prison number stenciled above the left shirt pocket. With his long face and balding head, he looked healthier than I had seen him in years. His attitude was dignified and subdued. Self-possessed, I guess. A fairly ordinary guy, I thought, mid-30s, who had lost his wife, family, everything material, and somehow survived with what looked like personal integrity. He got 1–15 years for a sex offense, specifically molestation of two young neighbor girls. Perhaps what I thought was dignity was stoicism, the result of having very little left to lose, and surviving the realization.

We talked freely and honestly and easily, during two three-hour visiting periods, and I was amazed at the change from the shy boy and man I remembered. Seeing him was a sad experience, but elevating too, because of his courage in the face of a dismal future. When I left I asked if it would bother him if our mother visited. "No," he said, "nothing bothers me anymore."

At the Motel 6 before turning the VW toward the threatening Rockies, I felt a wave of self pity for my uprooted state, triggered probably by my brother's predicament. I realized for a long time, not much had been fun or relaxing for me, everything had been sharp and hard and full of edges. No sense of quiet contentment, peace of mind, supper on the stove. I wondered if the smells of brewing coffee and frying bacon were in my future. Next, it was across Wyoming to Cheyenne and east across the long Nebraska stretch to the Missouri River, more or less going backward on the California/Oregon Trail.

◆   ◆   ◆

There's a Cheyenne intersection on Interstate 80 where you can turn to go south on I-25 to Denver or stay on 80. I had come through two years before after an Iowa City visit, headed west. This intersection, which for me had a mystical quality, was where you decided you were committed to the West Coast or you were going in some other direction. That snowy April afternoon two years before, I had stayed on 80 West, the Rockies in sight ahead, listening to Willie Nelson and Bob Dylan songs, and thought how great it felt to be back in the West and headed for the Coast. Away from Methodists, and low horizons and the vulgarity of nostalgia. Now, I was headed east and facing all these negatives, and uncertainty into the bargain. My immediate future was cheap motels and truck stop coffee.

My fears were overstated. Supper of catfish and beer at the American Legion Club in Lincoln with Uncle Les and Aunt Lorna and overnight at their house on S. 36th St. The next morning drinking coffee at the kitchen table, Uncle Lester, the official family historian, congratulated me for undertaking the Cedar County odyssey. The VW started at 22 below on that morning in early February and before I had thought much about what it would be like to be home again I was across the Missouri and driving with a 40-mile-an-hour tail wind through Iowa, admiring her winter dress of white and black.

I stopped at Newton for a cup of coffee and a piece of pie and pushed on to Iowa City. Off I-80, south on Dubuque Street, a right turn on Church and left on Clinton Street for old time's sake, past Old Capitol, the campus and the Airliner, right on Burlington, crossing the Iowa River, south on Riverside Drive. Suddenly I was home and they had to let me in. My parents were glad to see me, and supper was on the stove. I bellied up to a terrific meal of roast pork, mashed potatoes and gravy, green bean casserole with fried onion rings on top. For dessert, cherry pie with ice cream and Sanka.

I settled in for a few days of walking over to town, 15 minutes away across the river. Great fondness for my hometown surfaced. I realized how much I missed it when away for too long. I loved Iowa City, not because it was beautiful or romantic or mysterious but because it was part of me. The feeling had never gone away in spite of my frantic urge to leave in 1959 after college. I left that year, for San Francisco in a faded blue '49 Hudson. I sharply recalled the excitement that morning as Ken Weller and I headed west on U.S. 6. In spite of my youthful fickleness, I knew then that Iowa City was a good town, with a fine university, good cultural variety, things to do, intelligent conversations, a mix of urbane and highly educated people and dirt farmers in overalls. Thirty years later, it still was a civilized place, where cafes and libraries and bookstores were open on Sunday, where you could buy a *New York Times* and sit for hours reading at coffee shops. I was determined, though, not to let Hamburg Inn No.2, friendly beers at George's Buffet, the browsing room at the university library, walks along the Iowa River and home cooking divert me from my goal, which was to become an oral historian of Cedar County.

2

After a few days of living high on the hog in Iowa City, on a Sunday morning I drove to Tipton for a look around. I had imagined the scene a hundred times. The reality was not a lot different. Coming in from the south on Highway 38, the first sign of the town across the rolling country was the red-topped water tower. It was mid-February, and the fields were white and brown, but as a native I knew that by June, they would be green with new corn and soybeans and alfalfa.

In spite of the understated beauty of the countryside, first impressions were bleak, that Sunday in February. To quote my journal: "Well, there was a little snow, black trees, empty fields. The churches were busy. One traffic signal. Tipton looked familiar. At Zager Rexall Drugs the sign is gone, and the place is a tavern, but the Hardacre movie theater still stands across from courthouse square."

A few days later, I came back, rented a concrete block, white one-room place in a trailer court for $127.50 a month, including sewer, water and garbage pickup. They called it "an efficiency." In a previous existence, the little building with its lean-to carport had been the trailer court's launderette. The first person I talked to in town, an antique dealer on Cedar Street, was morose, and said I had come just in time because in two years Tipton would be dead. I left the warmth of my parents' house and became a resident of Tipton, Cedar County, Iowa.

◆   ◆   ◆

The first night in my converted launderette, I fought down rising sensations of anxiety caused by fear of the future. What lay ahead? Permanent unemployment? Celibacy? Eccentricity? Lunacy? After a supper of peanut butter sandwiches and Grape Nuts, I downed three cans of Old Style and hit the hay. In the morning, I put fear and doubts aside, buckled my armor and became a researcher.

My first stop was the public library, a neat-as-a-pin brick structure, slightly elevated, like a temple, set in the middle of a block of grass and trees on the south edge of the business district.

Back in 1875, said the history books, the area was noted for the health and longevity of its residents, due to a pure atmosphere, lack of local disease and evenness of temperature. "Ague and fevers are almost unknown."

Tipton, as described in A.T. Andreas' 1875 Illustrated Atlas of the State of Iowa: "The location is a very handsome and advantageous one, being upon a high, gently rolling prairie, surrounded by a tract of excellent farming land which has been well improved, and now presents as beautiful and attractive an agricultural scene as can be found in the state. The town is handsomely laid out with regular blocks, and wide, well-graded streets, and contains a number of elegant business blocks, handsome residences, good school buildings and eight churches."

In another description, done by the federal Soil Conservation Service, Cedar County was said to be a landscape generally characterized by low relief and a gently undulating surface, except along the main rivers, the Cedar and Wapsipinicon, where the landscape is rough and hilly. In some places the river flood plains are a mile wide. The highest point, about 960 feet, is in the northwest corner, and the lowest, about 630 feet, is in the south-central part where the Cedar River crosses the county boundary.

Annual precipitation usually is between 36 and 38 inches with an average seasonal snowfall of more than 30 inches. In winter the average temperature is about 23 degrees F., and summers average about 72. Winter days hitting 20 below zero are not unknown as are 100 degree days at the height of summer.

By 1988, the prairie hadn't changed. The "elegant business blocks" in Tipton had become less elegant and a few buildings stared back at you like skulls. Others had been diminished by tinny facades. The description about handsome residences held, for the town had many well-maintained Victorian houses on tree-lined streets. Churches, yes, and still eight of them, so busy that by city ordinance some streets were one-way on Sunday.

Tipton's population, based on current estimate, was 3,055, and stable. In 1871, it was 1,324, and in 1938, 2,145. Cedar County, according to the 1980 census, had 18,635 residents, and it hadn't grown much since then, given Iowa's population drain. In 1900, Cedar County's population was about 19,300. Almost all townships were losing population fast, except the ones with incorporated towns or near cities. In the 1875 atlas, the boundaries of the town were about what they were in 1988, except for the addition of some new housing on the north and northeast edges. As in 1875, you could stand about anywhere and see farmland. The fields come smack up to the edge of town, which from north to south was only about a mile long.

The formal history of the county and town had a couple of quirks, but generally the story was staid and predictable. Some gun fights occurred, and in 1857, lynch law and vigilantism held sway. Two horse thieves were hanged without benefit of jury. Whores, until controlled by forces for good, caused the usual distress.

First settled in the early 1830s, the county was named for the Cedar River, a pretty stream, and sizable, that angled southeastward through the southern part of the county. Tipton's namesake was a general from Indiana, a relative of one of the commissioner's who chose the town site in 1840. Cedar County was part of the Blackhawk Purchase, which grew out of the Blackhawk War of 1831–32, a bloody conflict the Indians lost. Some historians think this war was the proving ground for two officers, Abraham Lincoln and Jefferson Davis, who met again in grander circumstances.

Before the early 1830s, Iowa was strictly Indian Country and white settlement was forbidden. The first official government land sales in Cedar County were held in the 1830s after the end of the Blackhawk

War, and land sold for $1.25 an acre. A few pioneers were early birds, and picked off the best, thanks to squatter sovereignty. During this rush, eastern Iowa with its deep, rich soil typically was considered the choice part of the Mississippi Valley. East Coast newspaper advertisements that promoted settlement described the way local Indians, the Sauk and Fox, held up their hands when they first saw what became the Iowa country, and exclaimed, "I-O-W-A," which in their language meant something like: "This is the land."

Much earlier, this part of the New World had been visited by roving Algonquin Indians. French trappers and traders came in the 1600s. It was Indian territory after the Louisiana Purchase in 1803, and the main economic activity was fur trading with some business in buffalo tongues and bear and buffalo tallow, as well as pelts from buffalo, mink, skunk and otter. By the 1870s, the economy was based on a more prosaic and predictable base, specifically corn, wheat, oats and sorghum. A few crops were grown then that were not so important anymore, such as fruits, vegetables, grapes, tobacco, sweet potatoes and melons. The soil was described in the 1875 atlas as rich and dark "of great depth and fertility." Livestock production in those days was the same as today: hogs, cattle, and sheep. Cedar County early established itself as one of the richest farm areas in Iowa. It still was in 1988.

The quirky historical aspects all occurred a long time ago. One involved John Brown, the anti-slavery religious fanatic, some called him a martyr, known as "Old Brown" or "Osawatomie Brown of the Pottawatomie massacre." Brown, an easterner, was a firebrand who passed through Cedar County on occasion during his travels to and from Bloody Kansas in the 1850s, a time of great travail because Kansas was a pivotal state in the maneuvering between pro-slavery and abolitionist forces. He also was known in the county for his assistance in escorting escaped slaves to Canada on the Underground Railroad.

Springdale, stomping ground of my parental ancestors, along with nearby West Branch, had been settled to a large extent by fervent anti-slavery Quakers and those pacifistic people became close friends of the sometimes bloodthirsty John Brown. One Springdale Quaker was supposed to have told Brown: "Thou art welcome to tarry among us, but we have no use for thy guns."

One Cedar County story was about Brown and some dozen or so of his followers wintering near Springdale in 1857–8, and running a militia school at the William Maxson farm. Maxson (sometimes spelled Maxon), not a Quaker but fervently against slavery, was the grandfather of Floyd Maxson, who was my grandmother Nellie Bates Sanger's half-brother.

Brown spent most of the winter in the East soliciting money for his scheme to free the slaves. Back in winter quarters, his men drilled with hickory swords and fought sham battles in the hills near the Cedar River. Two Springdale boys, Edwin and Barclay Coppoc, eventually joined Brown's force. Edwin was hanged, as was Old Brown, after Brown's failed October, 1859, raid on the government arsenal at Harper's Ferry, West Virginia, one of the violent events leading to the Civil War. Barclay Coppoc died in the Civil War, and his name is on the white stone memorial to the Civil War dead that stands in front of the Tipton library.

The most famous Cedar County boy was Herbert Hoover, born and buried in West Branch, a town on the extreme western edge of the county. Hoover's history as famous engineer, humanitarian and one-term American president ('29–'33), although tainted a bit by the 1930's Depression, was treated with great official respect and federal largesse in the form of a national historic site and library. John Brown, disreputable but a major emotional force and a fascinating character in the days before the Civil War, officially was remembered vaguely, if at all. At an obscure country corner, there is a plaque on a rock where the Maxson farm was, noting the John Brown connection.

Otherwise, in a superficial and somewhat amateurish perusal of county history, about all I found of general interest was the Cedar County Cow War of 1931. A complicated mess, it had to do with local farmers' protests of state testing for bovine tuberculosis. Farmers complained about the price paid by the state for diseased cows, and said the tests damaged healthy cows and caused abortions. Some ugly scenes occurred, which resulted in two men going to prison. The National Guard was called out. After the Guard showed up, an oddly festive atmosphere prevailed in Tipton, and the tests proceeded without incident.

First prize in the bizarre story category should go to a woman named Mary Ann Sawyer. She came from England before the turn of the century and married an older man, a Tipton area farmer and dog raiser named Wickham. Shortly after she was married, Mrs. Wickham, in "a temperamental moment," went to bed and never got up again except, some say, to obey the call of nature and perhaps to play with her husband's dogs. They took her to the cemetery in 1930, some 40 years after her wedding.

With the Wickham story, I decided my formal research on Cedar County history was completed. Early on I decided my main technique would be to let Cedar County residents tell their story in their own words, and that my writing model would be a superb book called *Akenfield*, a portrait of an English village by Ronald Blythe. To cut the suspense short, during my Tipton sojourn I learned at least two things. I wasn't Ronald Blythe and Memory Lane had been replaced by Interstate 80.

3

As I settled into my concrete bunker close to winter's quiet fields, I noticed how quickly life became a series of familiar things. To the M&L Café across from the courthouse for coffee and a sweet roll one morning, to the Maid-Rite near my place on the next for coffee and a short stack. After 9, I check my post office box. I visit the library daily for historical research and magazine reading and a look at the new books. I walk everywhere, and notice almost no one else did. On warm days cattle were in the harvested corn and on a drive to Iowa City one afternoon I saw 30 hogs lolling on the sunny side of a barn.

I wrote friends in Seattle:

"Yes, I have a coffee spot. Two of them. The Maid-Rite and the M&L Café across from the courthouse. No espresso. I settle for a sweet roll and mud. They don't call them Danish here. I read the *Des Moines Register* or, if a Wednesday, the *Tipton Conservative and Advertiser*. The wind is blowing cold out of the northwest, corn and bean stubble is covered by snow, but the willows are barely beginning to show a bit of color. I am living in a concrete block building that rents for $125 a month, located in a trailer park at the northwest corner of this little county seat town, within a block of corn and soybean fields. Today, a strong wind is blowing from the west and the temperature is about 25 degrees. Snow has drifted high in the ditches and against the fences. When I drive to Iowa City I look at the white fields, blown bare and brown in places, the isolated and severe farm houses and barns, and get a feeling, unusual in my experience, that I am in the right place.

"I'm reasonably content and, although lonely, I have a strong sense I did the right thing in burying Seattle. I have experienced long and painful moments when I realize I left many familiar and good things behind, a sort of life. Even so, I have never regretted cutting the connection and ending the destructive banality of my former wage slave existence. I feel optimistic, not so much about this writing project because I know how ephemeral it is; I suppose it is the exhilaration of escape that feels so good.

"I have decided to let life here unfold at its own pace, with a nudge now and then from me. I will wait to learn the rhythm. One way is to hang out at the Maid-Rite and M&L, mostly the Maid-Rite because it's closer to me, keeps longer hours, and seems to have a greater diversity of clientele. I drink coffee and listen to conversations.

"I have learned that farmers like to drink coffee in the mornings and talk about sports, livestock, pesticides, the federal government, gambling in Vegas, bloody scours, Arizona, machinery, not necessarily in that order. Their affectionate, sometimes baffled, conversations about livestock I sometimes think are metaphors for the women in their lives. Every man wears a cap, usually with a trademark on it, varying from hybrid seed corn to a favorite herbicide or tractor. Except for waitresses, few women frequent the café.

"The conversation this morning was about pesticide regulations: a new law says anyone carrying pesticide, including farm wives and kids, has to have a chauffeur's license. That, along with the usual Arizona anecdotes. It seems as if half the people in the Maid-Rite at any given time have either returned recently from Arizona or are planning a trip there. Phoenix, Mesa, Scottsdale. Another topic is the upcoming NCAA basketball tournament, with people assuming that Iowa will stay in the tourney for a while.

Implement dealer Bob Jacobsen was there. On his way out, after exuberantly putting his arm around me, he said he was in the Maid-Rite every morning from 5:30 a.m. until 7, when he went to his dealership. Happiest time of the day because no one bothered him."

♦   ♦   ♦

One morning, I decided my research phase was over and the time had come to go into the field. The only person I had been in touch with before coming to Tipton was Gordon Esbeck, Tipton's mayor, a big, friendly man, taciturn, who made his living as a veterinarian. On a matchless day, warm and bright, the last one in February, middle-aged vets Doc Esbeck and his partner Dr. John Krob and yours truly drove in a Ford pickup, pulling a cattle chute on wheels, to Al Wright's mother's place east of Tipton for an afternoon of vaccinating and delousing 64 cows. On the way, Doc Krob told me what would happen. The aim was to get each cow singly into the narrow chute (called a squeeze chute because it had an adjustable gate at the head end) so the animal could be vaccinated against several possible bovine pregnancy-related problems, including venereal disease and spontaneous abortion. Each cow would get a shot to prevent scours, and a dose of systemic delouser which was poured directly on the cow's hide and subsequently absorbed. "Very effective," said John Krob.

Another purpose of the visit was to check for pregnancy in cows that didn't look "calf-ish." Krob had this duty, which he accomplished by rolling up his left sleeve, putting a thin plastic glove over his arm and shoving it into the cow's rectum up to his shoulder, then feeling around deep inside for signs of a calf. Krob also injected the medicines, using tools that resembled stapling guns with needles. The needles looked like props for a horror movie.

Esbeck handled the head gate, trapping the cow's head, and deftly cutting off her old numbered tag and attaching a new one with another stapling-gun like tool. Some bleeding was involved in this maneuver but the cows didn't seem to mind much. It took about 25 seconds per animal to complete the entire sequence, if the cow cooperated.

The Wright farm was well set up, with white barns, numerous pens for cattle and separate ones nearby for hogs. Great round bales of hay, each weighing 1,500 pounds and covered with black waterproof plastic lay a ways from the cattle yard. The day was warm and cumulus clouds were stacked in a very clear light blue sky. In the flat distance, red and white farm buildings dotted the fields in every direction. On hand to help were Wright's two grown sons, Kevin and Kerry. The work proceeded in a business-like way, with an occasional laconic witticism.

"Where's your bulls?" Krob asked, as he forced his left arm up to the shoulder inside a Hereford cow.

"Hamburger," replied Wright.

"So's this one. Nothing in her," said Krob.

"What's her number?" asked Wright, and failing to find his notebook, wrote 138 on the inside of his hand.

The work was muddy and strenuous. Wright and his sons usually had to force the cows, weighing more than a thousand pounds, into the chute. They pushed, swore, cajoled. One technique was to expertly twist the cow's tail over her back and sort of lift her in.

The vets earned their money when a mixed breed Angus and Hereford, weighing at least 1,400 pounds, was too wide for the chute and got wedged after losing her footing during a mighty lunge. Finally, after a lot of head scratching, Kerry brought a John Deere tractor into the yard, and a log chain was attached to the cow's neck and she was dragged out of the chute. For a while, as the cow sprawled in the mud unable to get up, exhausted, gasping and grunting for breath, it looked as if they would have to slit her throat.

"My freezer's already full of hamburger," Wright said. It was decided to wait a while, and before the other cows were finished, the imperiled cow regained her feet and joined the herd.

There was more trouble when another cow, by far the wildest of the herd, tried twice to climb out of the pen and jump over a low building, practically wrecking a section of fence and tearing up a length of tin roofing. Before she was finished, the animal slammed into a gate and sent Al Wright sprawling in the mud.

"Well the end of another episode of Wild Kingdom," said Kerry as the last cow was released from the squeeze chute.

◆   ◆   ◆

A few days later, Doc Esbeck asked me if I wanted to take another trip to the Wright place, this time to vaccinate pigs. I said sure, since I liked pigs and had fond memories of Stubs, a Berkshire female I had raised from a runt when I lived on the farm south of Tipton.

That morning, before going out with the vet on the hog vaccination assignment, I had the fascinating—but unsettling—experience of watching the castration of a bull calf. This particular calf had been missed during the routine castration screening at the sale barn, somehow slipping through the pre-sale scrutiny. Doc Krob said you could almost always tell a bull calf in an otherwise castrated steer herd because the animal stood out from his generally passive fellows. "Head up, looking around, acting cocky." I thought to myself that description fitted a few people in various city rooms I had worked in.

The young bull's testicles were about as big as a movie theater popcorn bag. Amazingly, the animal didn't flinch or make a sound as the razor-sharp tool did its quick work. The secret, I was told, was that while the vet was doing the cutting, another man twisted the bull's tail so expertly that the sensation of the tail twisting took the animal's attention away from the castration. The testicles were donated to the VFW or the American Legion, and frozen annual Rocky Mountain Oyster feed. Deep-fried, rich, and delicious, I was told.

By comparison, the hog vaccination was pretty staid, although my heart leaped when I went inside the hog house with 60 gilts (virgin females) and smelled the unforgettable odor of a hog house in winter. Heavily humid, not unpleasant, an instant time machine back to the days of Stubs, my 605-pound Berkshire female. The fate of Stubs was my first important lesson in agricultural reality. If a female pig can't reproduce, she goes to market no matter how pretty or smart or friendly. Stubs had become almost a pet, but after she turned out to be infertile, my dad, reluctantly and almost sadly, told me Stubs had to go. This comment meant a one-way ride to Wilson Packing in Cedar Rapids. Stubs sold for the astronomical sum of $106. I bought a nearly worthless pony, a saddle and cart with the money. I avoided bacon for several years.

After my Stubs reverie, Kerry, Kevin and I stood inside the hog house and talked about government programs, bankrupt farmers, runt pigs, the right kind of music to play in farrowing houses. They played WMT from Cedar Rapids, so they could get easygoing music as well as news and market reports. They liked the rapid development of hogs compared to cattle. A sow can have little pigs every four or five months, but a cow takes nine months from breeding to dropping the calf. I guess I never realized before how reproductive sex is practically the ball game in raising livestock. That and keeping them free of disabling disease, which lurks everywhere but is kept at bay by intelligence and modern veterinary medicine.

We also talked about farm troubles, and the upshot was that they thought a lot of the trouble was based on greed and mismanagement, as well as bad luck, falling prices, bank foreclosures and the like. The Wright boys weren't immune from financial disappointments. They had bought, with their dad, 160 acres during the height of the farm land price spiral, paying $3,000 an acre, with the land falling in value to $1,300. They weren't bitter. Both were relaxed and apparently happy with their lot. They liked raising pigs, and were almost affectionate toward them, which wasn't hard because pigs are as smart or smarter than most dogs. A cynic might wonder how smart pigs really are, though, since their life is short and consists of putting on weight and making a one-way trip to the hog buying station.

◆   ◆   ◆

Doc Esbeck and I ran into Bob Jacobsen, the Massey-Ferguson dealer, at the Maid-Rite where we stopped for coffee after the vaccination morning. Jacobsen, 42, bought the dealership for a good price in 1985 in the trough of the farm troubles. He said conditions were much improved, although new equipment still wasn't selling well. But used stuff was selling and he went to nearby states looking for it.

His notion was that the harrowing economic times that had ended about two years before were not so much a catastrophe as an experience that made farmers and farm-related businesses aware of the way things were. They had to change, or go under. The unreality of good times could not last forever. He cited examples of farmers leaving he business, giving back land or down payments, or finding jobs off the farm and renting their land.

After the pick-me-up at the Maid-Rite, Doc Esbeck and I went to the Rotary luncheon at the country club. I was asked to explain to them what I was doing in Tipton. They laughed good-naturedly when I told them I was thinking about writing something about life in a country town.

One of the men at the Rotary lunch was Stuart Clark, editor of Tipton's weekly newspaper, the *Conservative and Advertiser*. The paper was run by Stuart, 32, and his dad, H.E. Clark, the publisher. H.E. was a hard-eyed, gray-bearded man of 69, sometimes preoccupied and aloof during subsequent meetings on various sidewalks. Stuart was personable and pragmatic. Publisher Clark for many years had lived on Ireland's Dingle Peninsula during all or part of the summer, which gave him a cosmopolitan style. My first talk with them was in a conference room in the 112-year-old well-maintained brick newspaper building near City Hall. Clark elder did most of the talking that day, although in later months Stuart and I often drank coffee at the M&L Café and talked of subjects other than Tipton and its society.

Father and son were reasonably optimistic about Tipton's future, although neither man had any illusions about the precarious economics of small towns in the Midwest. H.E. Clark, energetic and acerbic, had little patience with some Tipton residents he referred to as "prophets of doom." Tipton, said the elder Clark, was like a New England village, all closed up, until about 10 years after World War II. "If you weren't born here, you weren't anybody. But Tipton changed after the war, like everything else."

Stuart had lived in Tipton all his life, except for his time at the university in Iowa City, where he majored in social welfare and journalism. He planned to stay in Tipton to run the paper, although it was clear from an occasional wistful look or comment during our coffee meetings that he might have other plans if he weren't the son of the publisher. His four siblings had moved away.

Stuart's dad had mentioned that Tipton had been a closed up town years ago, and I had been told the town still was not particularly friendly to newcomers. I decided to go talk to an old-timer.

◆   ◆   ◆

Mary Betty Huber was 77, Tipton born, the daughter of an osteopath who had migrated from Missouri. She lived in a large and comfortable two-story house on shady Walnut Street. A spirited and cultured woman who lived alone, she sat surrounded by books and landscapes done in oil, painted by her artistic mother. Mrs. Huber walked with a cane and at the time of the interview was recovering from cataract surgery. I asked her to sketch her life history and she did, willingly, and with good humor.

"It's a nice place to live. Of course, I wandered. I grew up across the street. We lived there until I was graduated from the university in Iowa City, with a major in history and political science. The year I graduated, 1933, our mother's aunt lived up the street, across from the United Church, where the funeral home is now. She was dying of cancer, so mother went up to take care of her. '33 was a bad time to get a job, and they called me and asked me to work for the newspaper here in Tipton. I wasn't interested in any thing like that, but I labored there for a year. Then, I went to Chicago to take shorthand and so on, and came back here. My aunt and uncle in California invited me out there, maybe you'll have better luck out there, they said. I lived there and worked for the Southern California Gas Company in Los Angeles. Part of the time downtown, and later I was a branch manager in the northeast part of the city. It was much different than it is now. I would be scared to death out there now. I was there for five years.

"I married a fellow from here. He came out to California and we were married out there. He was an attorney, who kept moving around. He hadn't practiced for quite a while. We lived part of the time in Tipton and part of the time in Texas and Arizona and so on. We lived off his investments. I had some back surgery and he left. (She laughed after this remark.) I knew where he was but he didn't come back. Anyway, after that, I went back to school at Iowa and got a master's degree in English. I taught and was a librarian at the junior and senior high schools here. I retired in 1967. I took care of my mother then until she died. I never remarried."

Mrs. Huber was very fond of her brother, Bill Furnish, a retired geology professor at Iowa who lived in Cedar County across the river and up a hill from the hamlet of Rochester. Bill was a working geologist for many years all over the world for oil companies until he came home to teach at the university in Iowa City. I knew him because he was one of the people I went to gun shows with, when an old high school buddy of mine got up a van pool for a distant show.

Mrs. Huber continued:

"Well, I used to watch the Tipton population. And it was 2,500 for a long time, it didn't change much. Now, it's a few over 3,000. At one time, a new house around here was quite something. I lived across the street when this house was built, I think in 1920. I have too much house. I live on one floor.

"You know, it's strange, Fourth Street over here was the first paved street in the residential area. It was brick. There was quite a lot of traffic in the early days. It was the main route to Davenport. During the bootleg times, you would see cars going by with the springs way down by the paving. In fact, we did have some difficulty a couple of times. They stopped them outside of town and one of our local fellows, a vigilante I guess he would have been, was helping out the sheriff and he was killed. Mother used to worry. We sat out in front and wrote down the license plates of every car that went through. That was in the '20s.

"The town has a few more people now, but it's not too different. We have a couple of manufacturing places here now, that's new. And quite a few people have moved here to live but they work in towns around here, like Cedar Rapids, Davenport, Muscatine, Iowa City and so on. They want to live here because it is a good place to raise a family. I feel perfectly secure here living alone, and I wouldn't very many places now. I think I would be scared to death out in Los Angeles.

"We in Iowa always think we should get to greener pastures, don't we? When I graduated from college, I thought if I could just go into Chicago, that would be heaven. Well, about eight months, that was enough. I've done a little traveling in recent years, I've been to New York a couple of times and gone to shows, a cruise to South America, but I am getting very much to the point where I am staying home. I am losing my friends. There are a few around I went to school with, from way back when. I have a bridge club and a couple of social clubs, and with the church that keeps me busy enough. We're blessed here, with being so near Iowa City and Hancher Auditorium. We get some wonderful things. There have been five of us going over there for concerts and various things, such as the Joffrey Ballet. And the hospitals at Iowa City have meant a lot to me, maybe a little too much."

◆   ◆   ◆

I talked to Judith Wacha, a newcomer to Tipton, in the early morning of a day in late June. We started a few minutes after 6 because we
wanted to beat the merciless heat and humidity of an Iowa summer
day. We sat at a little table on the front porch of her big white house
on a spacious corner lot two blocks north of the post office. She served
hot coffee with a slight chocolate taste, and sponge cake. About 40
years old, a plain, fit, forthright woman, she was wearing shorts and a
loose blouse, her graying hair tied up off her neck. On my bicycle rides
and walks to the post office, I often had seen her in the large yard,
mowing grass, trimming or planting. Always alone, by preference, I
learned.

My meeting with Judith Wacha occurred long after I talked to Mrs.
Huber, and by the time of the early breakfast on West Eighth Street I
was more familiar with Tipton. The Wacha breakfast chat indicated
another way of looking at Tipton, from the perspective of an educated
and intelligent newcomer. An Iowan but not a Tiptonian.

Judith grew up in Toledo, a small town in central Iowa, a bit smaller
than Tipton. She was bored in her hometown because of a lack of
intellectual stimulation, where cruising Main Street and eating giant
french fries at the Trojan Inn were the main pursuits. Something like
cruising Tipton's Cedar Street and eating french fries at the Dairy
Queen or pizzas at Happy Joe's. It was the kind of town, she said,
where wrecked cars were placed on exhibit and everyone drives by and
gawks. This example of small town Americana reminded me of Iowa
City in the 1950s when the U-Smash 'Em I Fix 'Em lot attracted high
school students after fatal accidents. A friend yelled one night, "Look a
little closer, you might see some blood!"

After high school graduation in 1965, Ms. Wacha attended the University of Iowa for a while, then she decided she wanted to be an airline
stewardess. This goal included going to a "finishing school" in Chicago

for one month. "Wow, what a big step, Toledo to Chicago. Petrified, scared to death. We were living in the Hotel Maryland near Rush Street; I was scared to walk to the deli." The stewardess possibility came to nothing, and she worked at Marshall Field as a secretary in budget shoes, for five months. She moved back with her parents, who had moved to Grinnell. Later, she lived in Des Moines, and worked as a secretary at Armstrong Rubber and was appalled at the coarseness of the men in the office.

Eventually, she returned to Iowa City and got a general studies degree. She took a 24-month radiology program at the university and moved to Chapel Hill, N.C., in 1973, to work in radiology. "I didn't do well out of Iowa; I don't know exactly why. I was miserable in North Carolina. The people were friendly, but they called me Yankee. Yankee this and Yankee that." She finally took a position as a dosimetrist at the University of Iowa Hospitals in Iowa City. "I decide how cancer patients should be treated with radiation working with CAT scans and computers."

Judith lived in Iowa City between 1973 and 1986, when she went to Tipton. "I had decided my life had pretty much come to a standstill in Iowa City. I was pretty much doing the same thing. The house I was living in was not what I wanted. I had kind of faced up to the fact that I probably would be a single woman all my life. In Iowa City, you meet a lot of people and make a lot of friends and they all move away. I have friends on each coast.

"Iowa City is an interesting place for someone who does not move. That someone was me. I moved mostly when I was really too young to learn anything from it, to have any good experience from it. I was too homesick, scared. Now, why I picked Tipton is strictly because of the house. I have a very strong homing instinct. I love real estate. I love to look at homes. Not for selling."

Her Tipton house, built in 1900, had character. Judith did not like it at first because it had an old people's feeling about it. She told the real estate agent she was not interested. A friend from Connecticut visited and she loved the house. "She couldn't believe I wasn't interested. 'This is the house for you, this is the house everyone would want.' I decided then I was interested."

The house was about as big as the Titanic, and even looked like a great white ship at night with the lights on.

"It has lots of rotted wood on the exterior but the inside is a real jewel. The downstairs is lovely. Or, you could view it as a white elephant. It is beyond my means to restore it. I paid $63,000 and it was not a good investment because it is in Tipton." The daily commute in her Volvo sedan is an hour door to door. "I drive 55, and enjoy the commute. It's relaxing. I take back roads, not I-80."

"I bought the house in November (1986) and moved in and my first reaction was I can't stay here, I can't stand it. Upstairs I have four bedrooms and a bath. The house seemed too big, it was winter then and it was bleak. I didn't know the town at all. I thought, 'My God, what possessed me?' But now everything's changed. I feel very comfortable in the house, it is just the right size. But, in terms of the town, the town has not changed in my eyes any, at all, but I am in Iowa City every single day, except sometimes on the weekend. I am a very fanatic bird watcher. In Iowa City living next to the cemetery and the park I had a million birds, and here you have very, very, very few. Number one, you don't have any dense cover. You have one tree in Tipton, the maple, not a large variety of trees, and that will cut down a bit on birds. Nobody plants bushes or flowers, nothing is here to invite birds. They stay outside town in the little wooded areas."

A red-headed woodpecker flew by. "Yes, I have three of them."

"I've met people here; I don't call them friends. I have no idea who these people are. I have been to block parties. What I do here is gardening. I don't do my shopping here. I don't buy groceries here. I don't buy gasoline here. The woman who lives over there (across the street), she is a younger woman, married to a chiropractor. She likes to walk and I like to walk too and we have talked about going walking together.

"A lot of married people and old people live in Tipton. When people get married something happens. You meet people with children and married, and when they find out you aren't married, that's it. I don't know if they are afraid for their husbands or what."

I asked if her neighbors would wonder who I was, sitting on her porch before 7 a.m. "Noses glued to the windows, you bet," she replied.

In view of her attitudes on Tipton, I asked her if the house were enough to sustain her.

"I am still doing a lot of soul searching on that question. I don't know if it is the newness of it, or if it is really the way I feel. And, if I am going to feel this way, being ambivalent about wanting to stay or not, my best choice is to leave. But I figure give it a few years. It took me a while to lash into Iowa City too. Social life for me in Iowa City was waning too. I wasn't a young college kid anymore. Iowa City is the best city in Iowa. If I moved, it would be back to Iowa City."

After the interview, she showed me her house, which was lovely, as she had said. Sparsely but tastefully furnished, meticulously clean and neat, an especially pretty wooden staircase, and there was a lot of good art on the walls. Her bedroom had little sleeping porches on two sides that provided cross ventilation.

Before I left, Judith said, on reflection, perhaps her own standoffish nature was a major factor in her sense of isolation in Tipton. "I'm basically anti-social, and sometimes don't answer my ringing telephone."

Many nights, as I walked by on my way downtown, I looked at Judith Wacha's white house. Almost always I would see her sitting in a rocking chair, watching her big color TV, rocking in short, quick movements.

4

Mrs. Huber was such a lively and upbeat interview, I figured maybe the older residents were the way to go. They could provide breadth of knowledge about Tipton and Cedar County as well as old-timer wisdom. I asked around and everybody said, "If you want history, talk to Martha Jane Henry."

On a rainy afternoon in March I called on Mrs. Henry, at her white frame house on Plum Street where she had lived since 1937, the year she was married. Her residence was across the street from the school where she taught social studies much of her life. At first the 80-year-old woman was stiff and slightly suspicious. She loosened up after I showed interest in her membership in the Daughters of the American Revolution.

Her only physical complaint was bad knees, the only way she felt her age. She had decided to see the world she had taught about, and had traveled the globe by ocean liner. To China twice, to Europe. Mrs. Henry had been a widow for 21 years.

Her father was an Army infantry lieutenant in the Spanish-American war, and his sword hung over the fireplace. During his 13 months in Cuba, he became acquainted with Col. Teddy Roosevelt. Mrs. Henry's dad became an embalmer after Cuba. Her grandfather ran a shoe shop in Tipton, after he came to Iowa in 1867 from Scotland. During part of the interview, a Bearcat police and fire scanner, one of Mrs. Henry's hobbies, was squawking. She listened only to the Tipton and Cedar County calls. She did not have children, saying "My children were all over there," and gesturing toward the building across the street where she taught junior high school students for 40 years.

"I liked the age group because it is a maturing time. Some days the youngsters were small kids, and the next day they came to school acting like adults. It was a challenge to me to meet the needs of youngsters at this time of their growth, both physical and mental. I taught English and social studies the first year, and gradually as teachers resigned, I got into social studies and taught geography in the seventh grade, American history in the eighth grade and civics in the ninth grade.

"My connection with the DAR goes back through Calvin Coolidge, through the Heywood family, or sometimes spelled Haywood. The Mayflower connection goes back to John Quincy Adams and John Adams, and back to, I think, Bradford or Brewster."

Mrs. Henry was an authority on Cedar County history and said the county "doesn't have to take a back seat when it comes to local and national history. We have Herbert Hoover's birthplace, but a lot of people don't know about John Brown and how we were an active part of the Underground Railroad. That was interesting to kids, the Civil War period and the Underground Railroad."

She didn't have anything good to say about contemporary treatment of historical subjects in Tipton, and she had one special pet peeve when it came to civic neglect. "Our town should be ashamed of itself for not doing more about education because in our town we had the first graded school west of the Mississippi River. That means up to that time schools had all the grades in one room, and they were not graded. And we had the first high school (1856) west of the Mississippi. The original high school is located just southeast of the library. The walls are plastered over the original blackboards. It's a residence now and not very well kept up. There is a bronze plaque on the northeast corner that tells the history, and there's a boulder with a plaque on the corner. People have tried, but not very hard, to renovate the house, but people get staggered with the cost and they quit. But, we really have something."

To get children interested in county history, she arranged for school bus tours and later adults got interested in going along. "We usually started near Springdale where John Brown was. The William Maxson house where John Brown and his men stayed is no longer there, but you can see the spot because they built a double garage where the house was. The Maxsons never cared if you roamed through it. And your imagination would go hog wild. People never believe in preserving things like that. They don't think there is any mystery.

"Then, on this little tour, we would go to Rochester, which was at one time our county seat. Rochester had the second bridge across the Cedar River. Another thing, in the early days, some men found there was silver in the soil around Rochester. There was a great deal of excitement. I knew where one of the mines was. It's gone now. They found getting $1 of silver out of the ground would cost $1,000. Their dreams went down pretty fast.

"Next we went to Cedar Valley, which was known for its limestone quarry, which provided stone for railroad bridges. I brought them around to Cedar Bluff, where the first bridge was. Another piece of interesting history about Cedar Bluff is that the Mormons from Nauvoo, Illinois, came up the river and bought six bushels of corn from a Mr. Gower, who owned the ferry.

"That tour was one of the things students remembered from going to school. I was the bane of a lot of teachers' existence. I believed children have to go to the place of excitement and enlarge their imagination. There's nothing duller than a kid without imagination."

I asked her what she had learned in 80 years. "Well, I think you always have to have a tomorrow. You make plans for doing something, and you live for the next big event. Another thing. I plan to stay in this house. They'll have to carry me out of it."

◆   ◆   ◆

Since I was pursuing the Tipton story using journalistic techniques, after two women I needed an elderly man for balance, preferably one with more of a rural background. Alvin Wright, the farmer I met during the cow and hog visits with Docs Esbeck and Krob, recommended his uncle. Charlie Wright, 94, horse trainer extraordinaire, was my man.

Mr. Wright lived at No. 2-D at the Senior Citizens' Park on the southeastern edge of town, across the street from a mausoleum-like factory which made little transformers for electrical appliances. His small apartment was clean and comfortable, and decorated mostly with photographs of himself and horses, models of horses and a glass case containing horse shoes Charlie had designed and made. In the kitchen over the sink was a plaque that said: "God grant me the serenity to accept the things I can't change, courage to change the things I can and wisdom to know the difference." A widower, Mr. Wright had been married three times. He had no children.

A native Kentuckian, thin and frail, he was a calm and dignified man in gold-rimmed glasses. His hair and trim mustache were white and he wore a western string tie with a turquoise center. He didn't want to talk about details of horse training because he was writing his own book, but did consent to talk about non-secret aspects of his life, which included remaining an active horse trainer until he was in his 70s. Iowa, he said, was a hell of a bad climate to train horses in, but if he had a choice between starving or freezing, he would choose freezing.

In 1911, he left Kentucky, knocked around some, breaking horses in Iowa and harvesting crops in Illinois. In 1916, he moved to Tipton. Mr. Wright was not at all interested in discussing the sociology of the town, either in 1916 or 1988; his interest was horses. Working with them was his life.

"There was a time here when the farmers said it don't pay to raise a colt. They shipped broncs in here, and some of them were pretty good horses. And a bronc is a horse that if you fight him, he'll fight you. That's the first thing most people do, a wild horse kicks at them, and they'll pick up something and whip him. He kicks at ya in the first place because he's scared of ya. The more times you whip him, the less confidence he has in human beings.

"Well, a carload of horses came in one day, and the farmers were told these horses were guaranteed to hitch. And the horse trader told the farmer who wanted to buy a horse what time to be there, and just before that he gave the horse a needle, and under dope the horse was draggy and accepted the hitch. I'm talking about smart horse traders. And the farmer would get the horse home and found out he had an outlaw. One winter I broke an even 60 head. These broncs came from Dakota, or wherever there was wild horses.

"One farmer said you better get Charlie to break your horses and the other farmer said he couldn't afford it. The first farmer said you can't afford NOT to get him. I had a system. I would get my wagon out in an open spot, of course I am telling you some stuff that will be in my book. The first hitch, well, just a rope going from the wagon to the halter. If the horse wanted to run, he had to pull the wagon with his nose. That didn't do any damage, but it was darned uncomfortable, and pretty soon the muscles in his neck got pretty darn sore. Nearly everything I did with a horse was something I had learned to do in my own way.

"The horse business was really busy in the winter time, up to the '20s, very few tractors then. If a farmer had a horse they didn't know what to do with, it kicked and bit, well, I was as important to the farmers as a good tractor mechanic is today. One Sunday a fella from Clarence came a-looking for me. I got $10 for working with a horse, and that's when a dollar was a dollar. Guaranteed they would start and stop by command, work on either side of the tongue, and you could pick up any foot and nail a shoe on it. This fella came down from Clarence and had his neighbor with him, and he asked, 'How much you getting?' The neighbor said he would walk from Clarence to Tipton to see a man put a harness on this particular horse. I said, 'Wait a minute, sounds like you got an outlaw. I might want a little more money.' I said, 'Fifteen dollars or nothing. If you're not happy when I get through, it won't cost you anything.'

"'Fair enough,' the fella said. He asked me what time I could come because he had promised all his neighbors they could come over and see this horse hitched.

"I got there about noon and his wife answered the door and I said I was the man here to break the horse. Well, she was all excited and I asked her to show me the horse because the husband was at a farm sale. She got a hold of him and he came home and by then I had one back leg snared. If you pull one hind leg off the floor, a horse can't strike nor kick either one. I worked with that horse until she wasn't afraid of me. I did one hitch and she grabbed the top of the manger and took a-hold like a bulldog and threw her head. If she had got hold of my arm, she woulda torn it off. I got her calmed down. But it would have taken two men to get her out to the wagon, and of course if that had happened, she would have kicked the front of the wagon out and still wouldn't have been broke.

"I went back the next day and worked with her some more and hitched her, and drove her over to the neighbors. I worked with her for a day and a half, and at the end, I could have nailed shoes on her. The neighbors said if they hadn't seen it, they wouldn't have believed it. It isn't bragging, but I think I had a gift for horses."

Only one kind of horse, said Charlie, can't be tamed and "that's a loco horse. In the West, there's a loco weed, and I've been told it's nothing more than marijuana and I've been told it's something else, so I don't know. One day I asked a fellow about a big plow horse, and the farmer said he was kind of funny. I said, maybe he needs a little work. This fella knew I guaranteed my work. He sent him down and I had that horse 10 days and couldn't teach him a thing. He was loco. He came from somewhere in the West."

Charlie Wright liked aphorisms. His favorite: "It's the horse makes the man, not the man makes the horse."

"One of the most important things is to get the horse's confidence. I say dealing with horses is like dealing with people. You don't care to deal with people you haven't got confidence in, and a horse don't care to work with a person unless he has confidence in him. To get the best out of a horse, the horse has gotta like you."

◆   ◆   ◆

After talking to Charlie Wright, I thought I had found my sea legs. A routine set in and life mellowed. I wrote friends letters that glowed with the rightness of things:

"Life, oddly enough, goes quite well. I'm semi-reclusive, and I work on my examination of rural life when I please. I talk to people, listen to conversations at the Maid-Rite and at the M&L Café, read the weekly newspaper.

"Winter has come back. A strong northwest wind, and temperatures in the teens, part of a big storm farther west in Nebraska and Wyoming. A flurry of snow now and then. The country maintains its austere bleak look. Brown tones with no trace of any bright color. I heard some women talking earlier in the week about seeing a bunch of robins. Early arrivals, probably, freezing now and cursing their luck. It was so warm last week, hogs were lying in the open, soaking up the sun."

A couple of cheery letters, though, didn't mean a spring-like mood had come to stay. A few days later I wrote in my journal: "Bedeviled tonight by doubts, brought on by loneliness. I wonder if loneliness is a virus that suppresses the emotional immune system and allows invasion by opportunistic diseases like doubt and fear?" Graham Greene wrote that "the need for companionship long outlasted the need for lust." I couldn't decide whether to agree with him, since I hadn't had access to either lately.

I drove over to visit a friend from high school and college, and toured his splendid new house set on five wooded acres. My old friend was happy and obviously prosperous, and I went away restless and amazed at the contrast between his house with wine cellar, six bedrooms and uncountable bathrooms with my one-room cinder block in the trailer court. I listened to jazz that night on the radio and went to bed thinking of San Francisco.

5

Charlie Wright's talk of horses sparked a memory. On the farm south of Tipton, we had two big work horses named Pick and Pat. One was white, the other a sorrel, I can't remember which was which. They were animals who seemed devoted to each other. One of them gorged on new grass and was hit by a terrible case of colic, that is, he developed a near-terminal case of indigestion. The common remedy was to prevent a colic-stricken animal from lying down. The horse might kick himself, trying to dislodge the pain, and in so doing often injure himself or twist an intestine, a life-threatening problem. This horse was way too big for any human to hold up, so his partner did, leaning against him all night.

I told this charming story to no-nonsense Doc Krob. He was skeptical that one horse would have compassion for another, but agreed that it was possible one horse might lean on the other in a tight stall.

These two big friendly animals were family favorites, even though they were used less and less and seemed to eat more and more. One day my dad apparently realized the age of tractors had arrived and the need for horses had almost vanished. In another of those agonizing and unavoidable decisions, Pick and Pat were sold for dog food. When the truck came for them, we all stood in the barnyard, trying not to look at each other, hiding our tears.

By now it was mid-March. The engine of my momentum was missing on a couple of cylinders and the attraction of my solitary Cedar County life was losing force. Not quickly, more like a slow leak. Creeping ennui had come to call at the converted launderette on Lynn Street. Perhaps, I thought, visiting the Cedar County farm again would cheer me up, light a small fire. I had stopped by a few times over the years, and knew the house was gone, along with the windmill, hog house and chicken house, machine shed, all vanished. I went back again that day and parked at the closed and padlocked gate and looked at the place and let my memory wander back to '45. I could see the house, two stories, white and square. Only a slight depression was left where the house had stood, but the yard and a few trees remained, and I remembered my 3-year-old brother Duane and I playing in a yard-bound submarine, made of scrap lumber and junk furniture, war movie-inspired.

I looked for any sign of the shed near the house, used mostly for keeping odds and ends of tools, maybe some small machinery. I found a bayonet in the shed which I convinced myself was of Civil War vintage. It was a classy piece, with Solingen, the name of a German steel company, inscribed near the grip. I packed it around, but lost it between college and my first marriage.

In imagination I located the privy, which we called "the outdoor toilet," and recalled smelly chamber pots in our wintertime bedrooms at night, and emptying them in the morning. One memory, sharp as a photograph, called back the winter Sunday morning my dad, dressed in his best and only suit, was carrying a full, steaming pot to the outdoor toilet. He slipped on a patch of ice, but with athletic foot work, he managed to keep his balance while, brilliantly, he swung the pot in a wide circle, relying on centrifugal force to avoid disaster. The feat was one of my dad's unbelievable moments.

At our series of tenant farms, we seldom had the luxury of indoor plumbing. Usually the houses had only running cold water pumped from a well. We heated water on the stove for weekly baths in a round galvanized metal tub. Usually, though, we took sponge baths in the winter, a shortcut we raised to a domestic art. As late as 1952, a sophomore in high school, I was bathing in the galvanized tub once a week and carrying full chamber pots to the outdoor toilet shack in the winter. In the summer, you were expected to go outside when nature called.

Heating was usually a hand-fired coal furnace with one big grate in the middle of the living room floor. It was a luxury to stand on the grate while getting dressed on winter mornings. Sometimes all we had was a coal or wood burning stove.

After a while, the attempt to reconstruct the farm inside my head and heart failed, and I realized I was looking at a deserted farmstead, used mostly for grain storage in new metal bins. The only remnants of 1945 were the tumble-down tin-sided garage where my dad kept our battered '36 Hudson Terraplane, the tractor gas tank next to the garage, a remnant of the stock tank and two ramshackle corn cribs.

Looking at the barnyard, I remembered that after the war, my folks' discharged soldier and sailor friends and their wives and girl friends came to visit and stayed a few days, relaxing in the wonderful peace of an Iowa farm, posing for photographs in front of the barn, going for a spin on the Farmall, helping my mother in the kitchen and my dad with the morning and evening chores.

In fact, looking at this deserted barnyard, or what was left of it, was depressing. I left and drove south past the church, still in business, freshly painted and with a current notice board in front. I turned right for a mile on the gravel road and right again on a sandy dirt road. I stopped on top of a sand hill with an old busted windmill, a stock tank, a tumble-down shed and a good view. It must have been a farmstead once, with a house and barns. I listened to the rusty windmill squeak, and surveyed the scene which included pretty much the extreme south-eastern corner of Cedar County.

To the south and west, it was not changed much. Slightly undulating farmland stretching to the horizon. Looking east and north, though, the one-room country school was gone, replaced by a small factory that made load levelers for recreational vehicles. A big restaurant and service station, the Cove, had been built nearby to accompany the biggest change, which was Interstate 80, the transcontinental main street of the mid-continent, New York to San Francisco, never quiet, an artery of noisy diesel-plumed 18-wheelers, always restless, always moving.

The English poet A.E. Housman's poem about "those blue remembered hills" and "the land of lost content" could have been written about the view from this deserted sand hill, and I-80 had made Housman's "land of lost content" come true. The interstate highway had split farms, created dead-end roads, rearranged the landscape, shattered the country quiet. I guessed, though, that few complained much. I-80 was four lanes of federal all-weather road, fast and easy access to somewhere else.

Back I went to the launderette, after a cup of java and a piece of raisin pie at the Cove, for an evening of drinking Old Style and listening to jazz from KSUI in Iowa City. The music carried me to San Francisco and Mose Alison at the Sugarhill; Cal Tjader at the Blackhawk; Dakota Staton and Earl Garner at the Masonic.

◆   ◆   ◆

Life became linear. Lines drawn between my trailer park bunker and the morning ritual of Maid-Rite and post office, the afternoon library visit for *New Yorker*, *Smithsonian* and *Scientific American*. The angled shot to my folks' place in Iowa City. My interviews were a relentless, straight-ahead progression. In my daily routine, I had found a purity of line, an arid economy of form.

I opened a fortune cookie years before and read: "Conversation is a training for brilliance. Solitude is a school for genius." Sometimes I was optimistic enough to think so.

◆   ◆   ◆

Memories of horses had taken me to our old farm, and memories of the farm took me to Ken Muller's office to talk about modern agriculture. Muller was the county extension agent, the local farming information guru with a suite of offices in the basement of the post office. He also was my landlord since he owned the converted launderette and trailer park.

My knowledge of farming, based on my days as the son of a more or less transient tenant farmer/sharecropper in the 1940s, was romantic and filtered through memory, often an unreliable instrument. At the place south of Tipton we farmed 160 acres, using the medium-sized F-20 Farmall tractor for heavy work, and Pick and Pat for lighter, more delicate jobs, like hauling feed to livestock or plowing the house garden. We didn't have much else in the way of power or convenience. No combine, no mechanical corn picker. At harvest time for the corn, oats and beans, my dad either hired custom harvesters or traded work with other farmers who had corn pickers and combines.

Haying was the best, because in '45 we did it, really, in community, with almost as much handwork as mechanical. No hay balers. The alfalfa, clover or timothy was mowed, raked into windrows and picked up by a hay loader that used steel fingers to bring the hay onto a wagon, often drawn by horses, where it was stacked with a pitchfork. It was lifted inside the barn in great clumps by a fork on a rope and pulley, which ran on a track under the barn's roof peak. I was the kid who led the horse that pulled the mound of loose hay through the hay door into the barn, where it was released into "the mow."

The men doing "the mowing," the hay mow work, used pitchforks to distribute the load and then waited for the next. It was sweaty, dusty, hard work. I don't recall anyone saying they enjoyed it, but I did enjoy it, reveled in it, when I got the chance to do a man's work in the barn. Women worked in oven-like kitchens to prepare the noon meal, sometimes breakfast if the weather was too dry for much overnight dew and we could get into the field early.

By '45, most corn and oats and all the soybeans were harvested by mechanical corn pickers and combines. Horses were often used to "open" the fields for the corn pickers, which meant using horse-drawn wagons to pick a few rows at the ends of the field by hand so that the tractors and awkward pull-type machine pickers could turn at the ends of the rows without knocking down unpicked corn.

I picked some corn by hand as a boy, sometimes in the snow, a seemingly endless task, although I coped with the monotony by practicing a hook shot, perfected by a childhood hero, little Murray Weir, an All-American basketball player at Iowa. My hook shots were a theatrical and slow way to pick corn, and caused my dad endless exasperation because my hook shot, unlike Murray Wier's, often missed. We used horses because they would stop and go on whoa and giddy-up, something no tractor yet invented would do. No corn-picking hook shots into the horse-drawn wagon in 1988, no need with the huge four-row self-propelled pickers that cost more than a farm did in '45.

◆   ◆   ◆

Ken Muller, the county extension agent, was square-faced, studious, a careful man, 52 years old and connected with farming all his life. He had undergraduate and graduate degrees from Iowa State. His basement offices were scrupulously clean and organized, with files of agricultural bulletins and flyers. The offices had the cleaning fluid smell peculiar to federal government buildings.

"As an extension office, we're here as a source of information. We've become kind of a library: if you don't know where else to ask the question, ask the extension office. We deal with questions on all kinds of things, from insects to crops, farm programs, how to interpret the rules, how to figure out the best alternatives. We have an unplanned agenda, because we are constantly trying to find out what people want. We are constantly trying to get at the problem at hand, whether it's water quality or an issue of economics.

"Right now, in March, we're at the tail end of winter season. And winter season is meetings and information, so we're dealing with crop information, the farm program, because people have to make decisions on whether they sign on the line. And soil conservation has added a whole new dimension to farm programs. The farmer is obligated to be involved in conservation, so he's got lots of questions. Right now, we also are analyzing swine records. It's a time of year when a lot of record summaries have to be done. People are involved in completing a swine analysis of their operation. As we get down more into the spring, we'll get more involved in field projects, field plots.

"I work for Iowa State University. It's a three-way combination: the U.S. Department of Agriculture sends money to the extension system in the land grant universities, the land grant universities put that together with regents' money, the county has its tax base, so those three sources, but we do get one check from the state university and one from the county.

"I've been here in this county for 21 years. I came in as a youth worker from Linn County and became county extension director when the man here retired. I grew up in north-central Iowa, the Iowa Falls and Ackley area, on a farm.

"Our objective is to provide farmers and urban people with information in agriculture and community affairs, home economics, youth. Right now, a lot of effort is in water quality, to find out where the problems are. Also pesticides. A big push right now is to train farmers. They have to take a test and have a card that says he is certified to buy pesticides, herbicides, fungicide, rodenticide. You can't buy it without being certified. The test makes sure the farmer understands the label, calibration, general awareness. What he can do, can't do with the product."

I asked him how Cedar County was doing, how the county stacked up against other Iowa counties. "Cedar County agriculture is as good as anywhere in terms of productivity, in terms of people in the livestock game, cattle and hogs. Cattle shrunk, but then we went through a period of adjustment. This county was hit hard in the recession, a number of families had to readjust, reassess their economic situation. But it stabilized considerably with good money coming in from federal farm programs and money from livestock programs, quite rapidly this past year and a half. Low ebb was a few seasons ago.

"Here, families are strongly related. Land is fairly strongly held, but we still had a number of people who bought land at the wrong time and something went wrong. They got caught when economic conditions changed. When interest rates went way out of perspective. A fair number gave land back, gave up down payments, lost resources, a number of foreclosures. They go along quietly. Here, it wasn't in the magnitude of other places in Iowa. Some bankruptcies too, adjustments made quietly by financial institutions. When you go back two years ago, the attitude of facing up to these decisions, to back off, maybe even leave the profession and take a job somewhere else, getting the mindset that we will have to face these things and still have a good life. Well, people started talking about it and that relieved them of the agony and the cloud that hung over them."

Income, he said, came from crops and livestock, and farm program payments. During the past two years, about half the corn income came from government payments. Corn and soybeans were the leading crops, with hay, especially alfalfa, taking a good spurt lately for sale to dairy farms, horse farms and even zoos. In livestock, hogs were way ahead because they generate income faster than cattle. Sheep were being taken "more seriously" than a few years ago. Average farm size in the county was 390-plus acres, with heavy family ownership and no significant corporate ownership. Several farms exceeded 2,000 acres, but they were family operations.

"On a warm spring day like today, if you're a farmer, you start feeling that urge to look out there and think what has to be done next. You get itchy. The timing factor is very critical. The ground has to dry out. Days to get tillage done, anhydrous (fertilizer) supplied, get the seed out there early enough to get the best possible crop. In late April, we really are intent on being on our toes and getting things planted. Oats can go in fairly early, mid-March sometimes. When it comes to corn, the soil has to be warmer and the last week in April to the first week in May is probably the greatest period in which most corn is planted, and beans follow that because beans can't stand as many cold days in the soil. Some farmers get out in the fields when they are still frozen to spread fertilizer and lime.

"Land quality in the county is quite high. You look at land where we're sitting and go north, this is very high quality land. We have two rivers, and around them it's rougher with more timber and pasture land, but in general we have about as good a land as you can buy in the state of Iowa."

◆   ◆   ◆

Muller shared the suite of post office basement offices with Rhoda Barnhart, the home economist, and Lori Grimoskas, the 4-H youth worker.

Mrs. Barnhart, 54, was professionally crisp, a good-natured woman, born and raised on a farm in Delaware County and still living on a farm north of Springdale. She and her husband experienced personally the farm troubles of the mid-1980s but she preferred not to discuss it in detail, except to say they once had 600 acres and a hired man. By 1988, they had 360 acres which was rented to other farmers and her husband worked as a custodian at the Herbert Hoover Library in West Branch.

In her work, Mrs. Barnhart dealt with the human side of the extension service, meaning programs related to the home and family. "It's pretty broad. I've answered questions today about clothing, foods, small businesses. I work with 4-H, but it's more adult education. Right now, I am writing a newsletter. I am especially interested in parenting, and in helping families with their children off to a good start. One of my jobs is the elderly and their problems.

"Farmers pay into Social Security, but at a high rate. And often there is not a lot to pay on. They can't count on that. Most of us had the theory to put the money in our farm, and when we retire, we'll have that. But when the value decreases to a half or a third of what you thought you had, well, a lot of people will have a really hard time when the time comes. More and more farm families have someone employed off the farm, and the kind of a jobs that many of the wives can pick up are low paying and don't have much in the way of benefits. What brought it to mind was that I was visiting with a farmer the other day, and he said he paid as little into Social Security as he could because he couldn't afford it, and said he would worry about retirement when that time comes. "My farm is supposed to help me get through that," he said.

"Things, economically, are getting better for some people. But it's real discouraging to the ones who can't see the light at the end of the tunnel to hear how much better it is. There was a time there for a few years when it was talked about so much that people were a little more ready to come out and say I've got a problem, which farmers are very reluctant to do, but I think with the climate the way it is, people thinking it's better, the ones still struggling aren't gonna be as ready to talk. The emotions they have been going through, and been going through for a long time, that's the hardest thing. They can be struggling for years and years, trying to figure out a way to make things work. They may end up in bankruptcy. They may end up turning it around. It may be getting better for people who realized they had to make a drastic change. Sometimes by selling some of their assets, if they were carrying a heavy debt load, that was one of the critical factors. If they could make some change and get that debt load down, so they could service it, then I think there is a chance. If they let it keep eating away, it mushrooms. It's like the national debt. Every year the interest is incredibly big. Even giving it back was difficult, because it was considered a sale and they had to pay taxes.

"In our situation, we sold part of our land. My husband got a job in town, and we rent out the land we have left. Financially, that's much better than when we were trying to farm it because now we have dependable sources of income.

"One of the big changes I've noticed is that in this job we used to be very meeting oriented. We would have meetings and women would come and learn how to make drapes. Now it's pretty hard in the daytime to get women out because most of them are working away from home. So, the whole pattern of how families live has changed a lot. I guess you would say it is more urban, because so many leave the farm to go to work."

Asked if women were more independent, Mrs. Barnhart replied: "I think it is more complicated. In my last newsletter, I went into alternative sources of income. You'd be surprised, a number of people have called or dropped me a note asking for more information. Today, a woman said she had finally approached her husband about taking in sewing or mending, and he had some questions about taxes and so forth, but I got the feeling that she felt he would not approve of her doing that. A lot of women are more liberated than that now, but a lot of them, their husbands feel their place is in the home and they don't want their wives going some place else to work. That's changed a lot, especially with the younger generation, but with the older ones there's still quite a lot of that feeling yet. I know a woman who's an excellent bookkeeper, and would like to do it for somebody, but it dos not appeal to her husband. Maybe she helps him a lot outside, I don't know the details for his reasons.

"And it used to be that big families would help on the farm, but now if you're counting on kids for work there's the old saying that FFA doesn't mean Future Farmers of America. It means Fathers Farming Alone, because kids are so busy with outside activities like sports, and many times we feel we don't want to deprive our kids of anything, even though there's so much driving involved. Some families do keep their kids home and they do a tremendous amount of work and don't get involved in the community. I don't think farm families would have a lot of kids now just to depend on them for help. The cost of raising children is too high."

Farmers have to learn to adjust, she said, and reach out for diverse ways of making a living. "You know, many farmers have the feeling there is not much else they can do or want to do. I was talking to one the other day, we got to visiting, and he said, 'Well, I've looked at a lot of want ads, and I just don't know what I could do besides farm.' Really, when you get to an age, and you still want to live here, well, they had an opening for a custodian at the West Branch High School and they had over 70 well-qualified applicants, and not all local. Some came from several counties off who would more the next day if they got the job. Many, many people around here are employed at the university. They work in the physical plant, in the university hospital as custodians—it takes a lot of people to keep that place going.

"The farmer who told me he didn't think he could do anything else had come in here to ask about a horse show, but after that he got to talking about how close to bankruptcy he had come in the last year. He realized my husband and I had made a lot of changes, and sometimes you need somebody to talk to. I think sometimes they need someone to talk to who is not judgmental, and they know it is not going anywhere beyond you."

◆   ◆   ◆

Mrs. Barnhart dealt with the realities of emotional and financial trauma, while her colleague, Lori Grimoskas, 26, a vigorous blonde, had what seemed like a cheerier assignment working with young people in the 4-H program (Head, Hands, Heart, Health).

"The number of people in 4-H here (about 250) is definitely dropping off, but that is occurring everywhere. That is why 4-H is branching out. 4-H used to be for the farm kid. The numbers are down. Families are not having as many children. But there are societal reasons for the drop, it isn't simply population decline. Probably the majority have a rural background or rural ties. Most farm kids have livestock projects, but these are often combined with woodworking, creative arts, photography, anything they are interested in."

She emphasized that 4-H has felt the pressure of the times. "4-H has been around since the early 1900s. For girls, it used to be canning, food preservation-type things, and over the years as needs have changed, it has gotten into more difficult topics. It would be a lot easier to deal with canning rather than drug and alcohol abuse and teen suicide, some of the vital issues the 4-H program finds itself dealing with now."

Lori Grimoskas seemed happy and adjusted to her surroundings, as did many people I talked to in Tipton. In her case, she grew up in a small Iowa town, got a degree at Iowa State in 1984. Her husband is Dick Grimoskas, principal at Tipton's elementary school. They moved to Tipton in 1987.

"I don't see my husband and me staying here for the rest of time. But Tipton is a nice community to move into. Dick and I have found it a real friendly community. Dick grew up in the Quad Cities, and a town the size of Tipton is a real change for him. He grew up with the Golden Arches right down the street and he could stop by anytime. We would like to raise a family in a town about the size of Tipton, and we enjoy being close to Iowa City and Cedar Rapids and the Quad Cities, and being able to go to those places for entertainment, cultural events, shopping, whatever, on a fairly regular basis."

The Grimoskas were Catholic, and I asked how important church membership was as a social force. "I think the church and activities have a greater importance and pull for some people. Coming from a small town, church activities were important. It was kind of like any other activity. Going to church in the Quad Cities was different than back home. You go to church and you leave. But here, in a small town, you go to church and meet someone you know, and you talk."

6

Personally, I was not religious. I was not philosophically deep enough or sufficiently aggressive intellectually to call myself an atheist. Non-believer was more like it. A secular person. When I read the *Mosquito Coast* by Paul Theroux I grinned in agreement with the sarcastic comment that "faith is when you believe in something you know isn't true."

My parents were not religious. They belonged to a fancy Presbyterian church but not for religious reasons. They liked the people in the congregation and enjoyed the social prestige of hanging out with brain surgeons and rich lawyers.

I had been slightly religious in high school when I joined the Methodist Youth Fellowship at First Methodist in Iowa City. Mostly though I was in MYF because it provided a chance to spend time with girls. My brother Duane and I had been baptized Methodists and kept our baptismal cards in case there was anything to it. We thought we could present them at the Pearly Gates, like a union card.

By religion, I am referring, I suppose, to Christianity, but since I'm broad minded I'll include the followers of Judaism and Islam. I didn't run into anything but followers of Christ in Tipton.

In my opinion, religion is a blend of truth, myth and superstition, not necessarily in that order. Religious rituals vary from something beautiful to tiresome mumbo-jumbo. Often I have wondered why certain people are religious. I have assumed social or family pressure was involved. Others were harder to figure. Faith, I suppose.

I admit I lack religious experience and my notions are pretty primitive. Likely, I would be laughed at by serious students of the subject.

I admired the humanitarian works of some religious people. Nursing nuns, for instance. It was obvious that the pastoral duties of ministers, rabbis and priests bring solace and comfort to many. The Ten Commandments, although mostly self evident, provided a basically decent approach to living one's life. I didn't follow all of them, including the one detailed in Ex. 20:17 and Deut. 5:21. I considered the St. James Bible to be literature, and even readable in places. I quoted from it whenever possible, especially from Ecclesiastes.

I liked a lot of men of the cloth, particularly priests educated by the Jesuits. I usually found rabbis to be sensible men and good conversationalists. I liked what one rabbi said: "We are punished by our sins, not for our sins." One of my oldest and best friends from college days, Jack Pereboom, was a Presbyterian minister in Illinois. He was a good person, deeply Christian in the best sense.

Clerics, in my experience, tended to be talkative, articulate and well informed. Good interview subjects. I felt that, in theory, at least, priests, ministers and rabbis were dealing with matters far beyond the utilitarian chores of auto mechanics and newspaper reporters. Cosmic aspects. Morality, death, what comes after.

◆   ◆   ◆

The Rev. Joseph P. Hines, 69, was known as "Father Joe" to his St. Mary's Catholic Church parishioners. Wearing black Adidas walking shoes with his priestly garb, Father Joe was a straightforward man who, at first, was baffled by my presence in Tipton. After I explained I was like a reporter working on a story, he was less baffled but no less suspicious. My guess was his experiences with reporters had not been rewarding.

Father Joe had served in Tipton for seven years, following 10 years as a pastor at Fort Madison, Iowa. Before that, he spent 10 years as assistant at the cathedral in Davenport. He was born and raised in Pittsburgh, went to Duquesne University, and to St. Mary's Seminary at Emmitsburg, Md., graduating in 1945. His first assignment was to St. Wenceslaus in Iowa City, 1945–50. He liked the idea of going to

Iowa City partly because it was on the same latitude as Pittsburgh. It would be similar in climate, and wasn't too far from his hometown.

The Tipton parish membership was 280 families, the largest congregation in Tipton. How come? "Well it would be easy to say, 'Me,'" he replied with a rare grin. The parish was small until the 1950s, then began to grow as people moved in. The Catholic population of Iowa, he said, was about 10 percent of the population, and in Cedar County until fairly recently was about 8 percent of the total. But for some reason, Catholics in the county had increased 12 percent. St. Mary's parish stretched for 10 miles in every direction, which meant about the entire county.

Asked how many members were farmers, Hines said in his estimation almost all were farmers, even people who weren't on the land, because everything in Tipton was farm-related. Implement dealers sold to farmers, auto dealers sold to farmers, the town was supported by farming. On the subject of the farm troubles, he was not charitable.

"Most of them brought it on themselves by stretching too far. Every business has failures. No one can assume success. Even if you've been farming for 50 years, that doesn't mean you know how."

He liked his work in Tipton. There was no Catholic school system, with the accompanying headaches of money raising and school discipline. The church was paid for, so he could devote almost his entire life to spiritual things. Masses, devotions, Catholic teachings. He preached three Masses on the weekend, and one daily Monday through Friday. Preparing sermons was his major job. He also managed the Catholic cemetery west of town.

"I preach every day. I teach a high school class and help out with the grade school children. I take confessions twice a week. Confession is not nearly as well attended as it was 30 years ago, but it is one of the most important things I do. I guess people have a looser view of things, and that's why attendance is not as high. People who do confess derive a great spiritual benefit. I do confessions in my office by appointment, and every year I get about 10 non-Catholics who are having a problem with their conscience. They are disturbed about something they have done or might do."

During the summer months two or three people a week came to his door asking for money. "They come to the Catholic church because they know the priest lives next door. They might say, 'My car broke down on the way to Aunt Minnie's funeral and I need a little money to fix it.' I would rather give them money or a meal ticket than hear a pack of lies. We have an emergency fund, and I give some of my own money too. I figure since I am deciding how much money to hand out, I can give some of my own, and make it one of my personal charities."

He did counseling, mostly marital and child/parent. "I never see any new problems. A child wants more rope than the parents can give. I use a non-directed technique so that I as the counselor don't become a crutch for the person needing help. I keep them talking until they come to a conclusion on their own. I encourage them to think it through themselves. It's a reflective system; I reflect the problem back to them and they solve it. Human nature hasn't changed. Everybody wants something it is difficult for them to have.

"It's the same things. A parent calls and says, 'My kid was driving around, and they were drinking beer, and he's in jail. Could you go down and talk to him?' I go down, and the kid's ashamed and doesn't want to look at me. But it's a peaceful existence here. If you don't want peacefulness, you can always go to Iowa City."

◆   ◆   ◆

At the other end of town, on Mulberry Street, was the First United Church of Christ, the Rev. Bob Molsberry, pastor. He was the father of two, 33 years old. Molsberry was something of a physical fitness nut (jogging and bicycling). He had served with the Peace Corps in Guatemala before his graduation from Yale Divinity School. He was assistant pastor in Aurora, Illinois for three years before coming to Tipton in 1985. Molsberry grew up in Grinnell, Iowa, and Iowa City, two college towns. His father was a professor of dentistry. Preacher Molsberry expected to stay in Tipton, his first senior position, at least 10 years.

Aurora, Illinois, his previous assignment, a city of 80,000 west of Chicago, was one-third white, one-third black and one-third Hispanic. Molsberry called it "a neat mix. The whites didn't think so, but it was good living in that kind of environment." He liked Aurora's variety, intellectual and cultural, including mundane aspects such as a wider variety of food.

The young pastor made a splash in Tipton's weekly paper right before Christmas, 1987, when the Rev. Jesse Jackson was invited to give a sermon at Molsberry's church. Later, Molsberry said the experience was the highlight of his parish ministry. The visit caused dissension because some in the 500-member congregation did not feel a politician should preach on Sunday morning.

"There were 400 people here when Jackson spoke. Probably 200 or more were our members, and there was a standing ovation when he was through, which was very uncharacteristic. There was this outpouring of emotion. After he was gone, there was some talk, but then it finally disappeared, like it never happened.

"This is not a liberal church. They wouldn't like the label 'liberal.' Now theologically, we are very open and liberal, but I am not going to say we are a liberal church because people would think that meant liberal politically."

The conversation got around to life in Tipton, his personal and family life, not his professional experience. "We find it is not what we are used to, and we are not comfortable. We almost have to approach it with the cross-cultural skills we learned in Guatemala. It seems like everybody our age has been here since birth, are entrenched here, and the things they are interested in are things we don't really understand, and we are not included. We hear time and time again it's a very cliquish town, very closed. I have talked to people who have lived here for 30 years who still feel like outsiders. It seems like people have their things going on and they don't go out of their way to include anyone else. I believe there are, though, a lot of people interested in new things, expanding their horizons. We're discovering our close friends are sort of the periphery of the community. The oddballs, the outcasts, the newcomers. Most of the people who have been here forever aren't very close to us. I don't think anybody means it, but an outsider is an outsider.

"I talked to a guy recently, an older guy, who had lived for 83 years in his house, and still sleeps in the bedroom where he was born. I thought that was neat, and then I thought I had nothing in common with him. We couldn't sit down and talk about anything. He wouldn't understand where I had been and why, and I would have no way of understanding what motivates him, what interests him, what makes him get out of bed in the morning.

"Probably 50 percent of the population, maybe less, belongs to a church. It seems more important to belong to a church and come here when you need it. Easter, Christmas, baptism, wedding, funeral. It may not be a central part of your life. For every member, it's an important piece of the background. I mean, it's a place to come to when you need it. About a third of the membership comes every Sunday. Church is not the central place in their lives. They wouldn't think of coming to church for recreation or study.

"There is no frustration here in terms of the church work. Things are happening. Like increasing the levels of activities, more participation by the members, making the church a center of people's lives. The congregation has enough money for the church to do anything it wants, if the expenditure is justified."

◆   ◆   ◆

The Trinity Evangelical Lutheran Church building was old and white and wooden, not as new or affluent-looking as the other major churches in town. It had a stern country look, plain and squatty, not at all like the modern, contemporary United Church of Christ or St.

Mary's, or the moody brick pile of the Methodist Church down the block.

The Rev. Donald Sondrol was a friendly, kindly, somewhat shy man of 52, dressed in shades of brown, from his tweed jacket to his shoes. I talked to him in his office in a concrete block building next to the church. His residence was adjacent to the church, a square, white, two-story parsonage where he lived alone. When interviewed, Sondrol had been in Tipton for one year and a day. Trinity Lutheran had 310 members.

More thoughtful, perhaps, than most of my interview subjects, one of Sondrol's greatest pleasures was the time he spent studying, every other summer or so, in England. In 1988, he went to Oxford University for three weeks of North American studies.

His previous pulpit was in central Iowa, in Ogden, 25 miles west of Ames. Before that, he was in Dixon, a small town 20 miles east of Tipton. As a boy, he lived in Albert Lea, a farming town in southern Minnesota, and, for a time, on a farm in northern Iowa. He went to college at Carthage in western Illinois, and to seminary in Minneapolis. He had a master's degree from Montana State University.

The older people in his Tipton congregation were basically Schleswig-Holstein German. "They are a very different breed of cat, very independent. Those who came over from Germany came to avoid the draft and to get away from the church, the state church at least. I understand that once they applied to be a German-speaking state of the United States.

"We have one couple here in church who are first generation. They came from northern Germany as children. They still speak fine German and have nice accents. Otherwise, I would say the older people are second or third generation."

Asked for his opinion of Tipton society, Sondrol did not hesitate to speak his mind. "My perception of Tipton is that it is hard to break into. I find it very difficult. I put part of it down to their background, but also I found much the same thing in Ogden. Their strongest suit and weakest was the same thing, and that's the location. Here, it's nice to be close to Cedar Rapids, Davenport, and Iowa City, but when you are this close to cities you find enough to do that you really don't have to have a community where you live.

"I had a meeting last week, a church committee, and one person said they had been here 18 years and still don't feel at home. They feel that people have not gone out of their way. When I lived on the farm during the war we couldn't get enough gas to go anywhere. Rationing, lack of funds. Everything then was centered around the school and the church. Most all of the social functioning went on in those two places.

"I am still at the point in the job where I am getting acquainted and getting things done. I am not home that much. It's very hard to get connections made. But being as single as long as I have, I have built up a certain system of survival and the way I do things. Sunday is not my best day, and I try to avoid anything Sunday after services while I recoup. And that is the day most people will be social. Twenty-eight years ago I became violently ill on a chicken dinner, and if you don't eat chicken you're out of luck.

"I've never really encouraged my parishioners to invite me to dinner, so I take some responsibility. Otherwise, it's hard to set one place at a table instead of two. People like everything to be symmetrical.

"Visitations are how I spend a lot of my time. I like to visit. I turn into a pumpkin by 10 most nights, but I get up very early, 4 a.m., and get office work done, reading, get my sermonizing done, grab the mail, a couple of cups of coffee, read the paper by 9 or so."

A morning ritual for Sondrol was listening to National Public Radio news. "I only trust Bob Edwards to tell me the truth."

"My afternoons are usually visitations, my evenings are meetings. Visitations are going to hospitals, stopping by homes to talk, and drinking a great deal of coffee. I try to work in visitations at night too, at the church meetings. So far this year, I've had four funerals. Last year it was two. Two weddings last year, and two on deck for this year. I do some pre-marital counseling and a bit of other counseling, but that takes a while. This church has been here since 1895, and I am the 38th or 39th fulltime pastor."

Sondrol mentioned that he went to the M&L Café on Cedar Street almost every morning, and except for a couple of ladies from the church who say hello, few other customers said much. "I am not the type to go in and sit down and say I want to be your friend. I also think people notice I go in and grab the *Register* and have a cup of coffee at the counter and read the editorial pages and get up and leave. So maybe they are respecting my privacy. And yet at the same time, they have never really gone out of their way to talk. I belong to the Lions Club and only go to half the meetings because of scheduling conflicts. I get the feeling I am there primarily to say grace."

Later on, he and I ate breakfast together a few times at the M&L, and I noticed a certain distance between us and the rest of the customers. Not a lack of friendliness, more like wariness, but perhaps only indifference.

During one of our talks, Sondrol said something which has become one of my favorite memories of a Tipton conversation. We were talking about the upcoming presidential election, and about elections past. I told him I had seen Harry Truman in Iowa City during the 1948 whistle stop campaign. Sondrol said he hadn't been that lucky, but he had seen Thomas E. Dewey and his wife during the same campaign, also at a whistle stop, at Albert Lea, Minn. Sondrol didn't remember much about Dewey that day, but he had a vivid memory of Mrs. Dewey. Sondrol was a kid, and he was standing close to the train at eye level, so all he could see were Mrs. Dewey's legs as she stood on the open air platform at the rear of the last car. "I remember her legs. They were covered with freckles."

He had been around the Midwest as a country preacher for many years, so I asked him to talk about farmers and their reactions to economic travail.

"The farm crisis? I think part of it is, shall we say, chickens coming home to roost. They (rural people) had been so vehement against others in bad situations, and they suddenly found themselves in one, it was very difficult to handle. When you spend so much of your time condemning those who go on food stamps and welfare, and suddenly find yourself confronted with the same thing, it is very difficult. I remember my parents talking about the Depression, and the great sense of pride in that they never asked for help. This whole work ethic becomes a religion to the point where it is sinful to ask for help, sinful to admit failure or weakness. It is so hard to work with. And then with our particular theology, which is based on the idea that nothing is earned, you receive it as a gift, and for this kind of society, that's just miserably hard to get across.

"Years ago, I got used to the statement that no matter what a person is, they are a good person if they work hard. Work is equated with goodness. The nicest comment you can make about anyone is that they are a hard worker, no matter what kind of schnook they are in other ways. Then, something comes up and you no longer identify yourself with work, such as people at a nursing home. No wonder the death rate is so great, the number of people who die on the way to retirement in Florida or Texas simply because everything they have identified themselves with has been taken away. That's rough."

"Well, for fun, periodically, I meet with friends in the neighborhood, between here and Davenport. I'm an opera nut, so Saturday afternoons are spent with scores in front of the radio, listening to the university station.

"I go to Iowa City. I enjoy the university library, especially the browsing room, and I visit the bookstores, which I enjoy a great deal. Upon occasion, a concert or other activities over there, depending on the schedule here. Friday nights, during the season, are spent at Tipton High School football and basketball games. I enjoy them. My TV set died in October of '74, so that takes care of that problem. If there's a show I want to see and I think someone may enjoy it, I invite myself over."

Sondrol brought up a subject which intrigues visitors to Iowa and even natives like myself, and that is the Iowan preoccupation with sports, particularly college sports. In eastern Iowa the Iowa Hawkeye logo is everywhere. On T-shirts and jackets, in store windows, on vehicles and mail boxes and painted on windmill blades and sides of barns.

(Later, I found out these Hawk-a-holics in their black and gold Iowa garb are known as "bumblebees.")

"I find that around here people are Hawks to the point of almost nausea. This may be the one thing that holds them together. I find it is almost always the same. If they won, it's 'we' won, if they lost, it's 'they' lost. 'They' didn't do very well last night, but next time it might be, 'we' sure won, didn't 'we'?

Switching from sports to spirituality, Sondrol said he simply did not know how spiritual his congregation was. "I have never been a good judge of that. I think here, as at most places at this time, there is a good strong nucleus of attendance at services, at meetings, at whatever. Here, as anywhere else, I think often they are here if there's nothing else to do. I have to be honest that way. I suppose it reflects my own particular brand of spirituality. It's never been that identifiable, perhaps, but I am spiritual in my own way, and therefore, I can't identify other people's. I find that the people that I do get to know because I see them the most, we never discuss it per se, but I think they have a reasonable spiritual life. Around here I have not run into people who are saved and who never let you forget it.

"I think for most people, churches are nice to have when you need them. You have a daughter who's getting married, we have a church so we use it, or a place to bury mother."

◆   ◆   ◆

A half-block from the Lutheran Church was the United Methodist Church, and pastor Jerrold Swinton. The Rev. Swinton, a 10-year veteran of Tipton, ran a church with 550 members. With his U.S. Marine

Corps-style haircut and brisk manner, he gave me an impression of great self-confidence. Coincidentally, the 51-year-old Swinton turned out to be somebody unusual in my experience. He was a graduate in February, 1959, of the University of Iowa, in history. When he mentioned these facts, I realized he was a classmate of mine, with the same major, and the only person I had met in almost 30 years who had graduated from Iowa in history when I did, mid-year 1959. Although neither of us remembered the other, a check of my journal for 1958 showed we were acquainted then. We talked a while about Giles Constable, a distinguished professor of medieval history, a man Swinton especially admired.

A distinctive part of Swinton's church was the lighted bulletin board in the front yard which noted times of various services. It also carried homey sayings. All summer the lighted board said: "Better to be a square than move in the wrong circles." As fall came on, the word was changed to: "To kindle zeal in youth, give them something to die for!" Later, as winter approached, it said: "God doesn't let his steady customers down." And, at Christmas: "Is there room for Him in your inn?"

A married man, Swinton's personal life sounded comfortable. "I have a support group, the men's prayer group. Most of them have been here quite a while. A couple of teacher friends are close to me; teachers and clergy think a lot alike. They value education and are more world-minded. They are interested in ideas and music. We like to think of ourselves as not quite so provincial."

I asked if he thought Tipton were provincial. "That's a good question. People in Tipton have been around. An old woman who had lived here when I was appointed here 10 years ago, said Tipton is a very gracious community. I think she's right. There is a graciousness here, a willingness to let people be and not to cause people problems who don't think exactly like other people. In that sense, I really appreciate people here."

So, what to Molsberry and Sondrol was a somewhat standoffish, maybe clannish attitude, for Swinton was a dignified effort to allow people their privacy.

"Tipton," Swinton went on, "isn't provincial as much of Iowa is, like southern Iowa or northeastern Iowa. Not closed. I don't feel constrained, I don't feel I have to talk their language or have their ideas. No demands that I be like them. Politically, I favor the Democratic Party and 80 percent of our people here I know voted for Ronald Reagan both times. I say what I think."

Swinton came to Tipton from Wapello, a small town further south in Iowa. He went to Drew Seminary in Madison, New Jersey, and received a doctorate there. He has served small churches in Iowa and Missouri. His father was a school teacher in southeastern Iowa.

"Right now I am reading a lot of theology, and contemporary Bible material. Trying to get on top of contemporary movements in both Biblical interpretation and the world of theology, which is in quite a quandary at the present time, with increased pluralism in our culture. We have the same thing happening in Toffler's "Third Wave" book, you know, the plurality of options. He's really quite prophetic. I see the same thing happening in religion. Like a giant ice floe breaking up, where things are headed and where we are going.

"I am not terribly optimistic about western culture in general. It has no center core; it has no real identity. It has no common denominator. When you've got to look for things like the blowing up of the space craft and assassinations to get common denominators in the culture, they are few and far between.

"A lot of popular religion is narcissistic, what's in it for me. I mainly want integrity. If I give a sermon along those lines, people do talk about it. I have an ability to get inside of people. Some people don't like me, but they are a little afraid of me, so they don't bother me. They may think I will have more ideas than what they can deal with."

Swinton thought most people in Tipton, whether they went to church or not, considered themselves Christian. "From my perspective, much of it (their faith) is quite superficial. But the identity seems to be very important to them. I don't get much anti-clericalism or anti-church feelings. Over the years the churches have tried hard to serve people. This particular congregation does a lot for other people.

"People of Cedar County are a very proud people. That's the first thing I noticed when I came here. People don't seek professional help until they really have to, and often even then they don't, whether it's a problem with marriage or legal troubles. They wait too long, and try to tough it out themselves. People are reluctant to get counseling. I used to do more than I do now.

"The clergy is an interesting profession. I don't know any profession that has anything like its breadth. You cut through and across so many disciplines. It's really quite incredible."

7

A fter talking to men of the cloth, I turned to representatives of government, elected and otherwise. What I found out was that local government people had the same overall goals and problems in Tipton as anywhere else. They searched for revenue, then tried to spend money in ways that accomplished the greatest good but offended the fewest people. They worried about their sources of money and how conditions might change in ways that would knock their plans askew.

Tipton was a small town in the Midwest, so people had an omnipresent fear of economic stagnation, or worse. Ironically, when a new, strong economic force came to town, it was greeted with mixed reactions. The new force was Wal-Mart. The giant discount chain was successful in Tipton but was blamed for damaging existing businesses. Some said the lethargy of old-line merchants practically invited Wal-Mart to fill a vacuum; others said the little business people could not compete with a huge powerful chain and the whole thing was unfair and might lead to turning Tipton's downtown into a ghost town. But even people who railed against Wal-Mart shopped there. People came from miles around to take advantage of very low prices, and after shopping at Wal-Mart often stopped for lunch or bought gasoline in Tipton.

I went to city council meetings and found the members talked about the usual things: money, expenses, state and federal grants and the uncertainty thereof. The experience was pleasant because of the informality, which included coffee for everybody in the audience, and the habit of talking informally with members of the public during the meeting. Bob Snavely, the city coordinator, asked me at my first meeting to tell the council members what I was doing in Tipton. They listened politely. I walked home and a rabbit hopped across Lynn Street in front of me.

Later, in his office, Snavely, 56, told me Tipton's annual budget was slightly less than $5 million. The town employed 27 people, including four policemen. Tipton was not broke or even close. At the end of the year, it had a bank balance of more than $4 million. Snavely, who struck me as a diligent professional, said prospects were good for economic development, and suggested I talk to Walt Ferguson, president of the Tipton Economic Development Corporation, an independent group of local people.

Ferguson was a veteran of Washington, D.C., a former official at the federal Department of Agriculture. He was county chairman of the Democratic Party. "I think Tipton has held up better than most. We face the same problems, though. You look around and a lot of the business people are older, and unless they can bring in some new blood, well, I don't know. You can't compare Tipton to some other towns, which are dying. Tipton is going to do something about its future. The county seat gives the town a built-in base. Look at Washington, D.C."

This information was fine, but I needed a human touch. I decided Rita Sissel would be the ticket. She was a city council member council and was a lively presence on the nights I sat in the audience and watched the council in action.

The Sissels lived in a spacious old three-story house, remodeled and renovated, on East Fourth Street, Tipton's prestige boulevard. One of three women on the six-member council, Mrs. Sissel, 42, was beginning her second four-year term. (Later in the year, she resigned her seat after moving out of her district.) Her family included a husband and two daughters, one a freshman in college and the other in fourth grade.

As a girl, Mrs. Sissel had lived on a rented farm near Tipton. Her dad had a heart attack when she was seven and the family moved to town. Her mother taught country school, and her dad subsequently was elected to the county board of supervisors. After high school, she attended beauty school in Des Moines, lived in Davenport, and returned to Tipton. Her husband, Robert, got a job with an air conditioning manufacturer and they moved east, to West Chester, Pennsylvania, near Philadelphia. That was in '74. Then they moved near Lancaster, Pennsylvania, which was more like Tipton. The family lived in Pennsylvania four years, then moved to the Chicago area, but the goal always was to return to Tipton, which happened in 1980. Robert became a partner in a machine shop in Bennett, a town near Tipton. The main reason for coming back was to be close to their families, she said.

"After living out East for a while, I don't know, this just seemed like where we belonged. Living there was much different from what we were used to. I was going to say I didn't like the coldness of the people, but that wouldn't be fair because when we moved to Lancaster we felt a closeness, and that they really cared, more so than when we lived near Philadelphia. I liked the East because we could see so many things and do so many things in comparison to here. We could go to the Pocono Mountains in an hour, Philadelphia was close, you could go to New York in a couple three hours, Atlantic City, Washington, D.C. in a couple hours.

She agreed Tipton was a hard place to crack if you were new. "I don't totally understand why. I felt it when we came back, and I don't think it's done on purpose either. It's like you're not part of what's going on, unless you come in with a good contact or a hold on something in common with a certain bunch of people. It's hard for the school kids."

Another gripe was the town's attitude toward women in authority. "It may sound sexist, but this town is really not used to women being in charge of things, and some people are still not very receptive. I have found myself frustrated because of that."

Mrs. Sissel worked as an assistant of Walt Ferguson at the economic development office, and I asked her about a comment I heard when I first hit town. One of the older businessmen told me it was a good thing I had come when I had because in two years Tipton would be dead economically, partly because of the aggressiveness of the Wal-Mart discount store.

"I think it goes back to the '70s, when everything seemed wonderful and it seemed there would never be an end to it. I suppose our town isn't unique, in that our town had a kind of apathy. They had it made, nothing could happen to them. I don't think blaming Wal-Mart is unusual. I haven't lived in any other small town in the Midwest, so I can't say for sure. There's a lot of resentment to change in this town, particularly among people who have lived here and never lived anywhere else, born and raised here and they don't like things to be shifted around too much. They like their town the way it is. Well, it you leave it that way, it will be gone in two years. When Wal-Mart did come to town, we knew it would hurt Shultz's (a variety store which subsequently went out of business).

"Part of the problem here is the negative attitude of a lot of people. Getting people involved is like asking them to invest in a business," she said. After that comment, her husband joined us and we drank coffee in their very comfortable living room and talked about the Victorian restoration work they had done on the house.

◆   ◆   ◆

I talked to genial Keith Whitlatch, the Cedar County sheriff, on St. Patrick's Day. We got along well, perhaps because we were about the same age, and both of us had grown up as the sons of tenant farmers. Whitlatch was a Marine who had served at the USMC air station at Kaneohe, in Hawaii, during the late 1950s. I had lived near Kaneohe in the 60s, and we talked about the Windward side of Oahu.

Whitlatch retained a Marine Corps presence, a beefy man but in no way was he fat or slow. The sheriff had settled down after leaving the Marines, and lived on 31 acres at the old town site of Shiloh north of Tipton. He loved where he lived.

The sheriff was interested in Cedar County history. A vice president of the county historical society, his goal was to build an agricultural museum at the county fairgrounds. He and I got along and he invited me to a supper that night at the Lions Club, where he was in charge of the program. The Whitlatch conversation put me in a convivial mod and I stopped at Anderson's Inn for a glass of green beer.

That evening, Whitlatch and one of his deputies were waiting for me on the sidewalk outside the Masonic Temple where the Lions Club met. The sheriff was dressed in a gaudy St. Patrick's shamrock shirt as well as a yellow vest loaded with badges depicting various events, all connected with the Lions. He packed a pearl-handled revolver on his belt. The crowd in the basement of the Masonic Temple included some men I knew. A few raucous jokes were exchanged before women brought out a supper of pork roast, mashed potatoes and gravy and string beans. Delicious and served family style. Conversation at my table was about livestock prices and the imminent NCAA cage tourney.

Whitlatch presented the program, which was mostly a video of last summer's old-time oats harvest using an ancient binder (reaper), an F-20 Farmall tractor (like my dad's), a hay wagon and stationary threshing machine driven by a Hart-Parr tractor. The film demonstrated the technique of shocking the bundles and loading the wagon after the oats had dried for a few days. The film was well received by the Lions, many of whom were old men who remembered the days of binders and shocks. They good-naturedly critiqued the technique of the Future Farmers of America members in the film, and were quick to compliment the occasional old pro who appeared.

It was striking, the number of men needed to do the work. One on the tractor, one on the reaper, heaven knows how many to shock, and platoons for loading the wagon and running the thresher. Afterward, Whitlatch, his deputy and the sheriff's brother, Bob, the acting Tipton police chief, made pitches for the museum and the importance of preserving farm history.

◆   ◆   ◆

During the walk home, I realized I had never asked the sheriff anything about his occupational life, nothing about crime or violence. My attention was centered on him personally, and his interest in county and agricultural history. The same thing had occurred when I talked at great length with city manager Bob Snavely. I was more interested in Snavely's days as a public utility employee than I was with his role in 1988 Tipton. I figured my lack of interest in asking questions represented more leakage in my journalistic/oral history approach, which I was beginning to think was stilted and much like listening to ponderous programs on the BBC or NPR. Earnest, responsible, fairly boring and pretty much humorless.

Somewhere I had read the phrase "personal odyssey," and it caught my fancy. I began to wonder seriously if I should wind up the formal interviews, put away my tape recorder and notebook, and simply live in Tipton for a while, maybe get a part-time job and relax.

A fresh wind was beginning to blow off the summer to come. In a few days, I was to meet Bob and Christine Gelms, who lived in a mansion on East Fourth Street, and, at about the same time, I met young Conner Meade, the Dubliner, a guy I nicknamed "the Irish degenerate."

8

I met Christine first. Stuart Clark had mentioned her and Bob during our conversations while drinking coffee at the M&L Café. He said if I wanted to meet two of Tipton's most interesting people, I should look up the Gelms. I telephoned Christine one morning and she talked my ear off. I was surprised to find out she had been born in Brooklyn (New York, not Iowa) but had moved to Tipton as a young girl.

The next morning I walked the mile or so from the bunker to her house on East Fourth Street where she ran a bed & breakfast. The house itself was a magnificent Victorian, four stories tall, counting the tower, the most imposing place in town. It had 17 rooms and was 105 years old. Christine was only 37, a high energy, feisty and plain-speaking woman. She was dark haired and short, jumpy, fast talking, worldly and good-looking. I knew Tipton wouldn't be the same for me. I didn't stay long that first day. We had a cup of coffee at her kitchen table. We had a lot to talk about but she was getting ready for a luncheon and was behind in her work. When I left, I knew I had found somebody to talk to.

◆   ◆   ◆

Before I saw Christine again, I met Conner Meade, 23, an Irishman working for a while as a reporter at Stu Clark's paper. Conn, pale, dark-haired, fine-featured and small, became my only drinking partner. On our first night out, at the North Star Lounge next to the Hardacre Theater, I asked Conn what he did at night in Tipton. He looked at me with half a grin and replied: "This."

The same night, when we closed the Last Lap at 2 a.m. Conn put his head in his arms on the bar and said quietly, "I want to get laid, so bad." When he said that, for some reason, maybe it was the contrast, I remembered that the Last Lap tavern, back in 1945, was Zager's Rexall Drugs where I drank so many chocolate malts before heading for the Hardacre across the square.

Conn was brought to Tipton by Herb Clark, the *Conservative's* publisher. When Herb and his wife went to Ireland for their annual extended visit, they often talked a young Irish man or woman into coming back with them to be trainees at the Tipton paper.

Conn was not impressed by Tipton's lifestyle. One Friday night as we walked from one of the three taverns to the next one, he watched Tipton's motorized high school set drive ceaselessly and noisily up and down Cedar Street, the main drag.

"Why don't they go to Iowa City and get into some heavy drugs or sex, instead of this endless driving back and forth?" Conn envied them in a way because they had cars and access to brighter lights even if they didn't take advantage. He had no car and no driver's license, and not much money. He had only the North Star Lounge, the Last Lap and Anderson's, and his dream of eventually going home to Dublin.

On weekends he attended whatever was playing at the Hardacre, and after a while I went with him, even to bubble gum movies with 13-year-old stars. He was a memorable sight in town, a skinny little guy, always walking and wearing a headset plugged into a hard rock cassette. Conn told me he had played some football in Ireland. In spite of his lack of size he was lightning fast. He tried rugby but he was too small and the game was way too rough for him.

One afternoon as we were walking off an M&L lunch of sauerkraut and Polish sausage, Conn said Tipton people, in general, were reserved in ways you would not find in Ireland. People in Tipton rarely talked to him in casual conversation on the street as they would in Ireland. But in a tavern or at a party Tipton people had very few inhibitions. For instance, a few nights before he had been covering the Buddy

Holly party, and since he was a stranger taking notes, a woman assumed he was a private investigator checking up on her. With no hesitation, she told Conn she was having an affair with a married man and she thought that Conn with his notebook and camera had been hired by her lover's wife. Conn, a reader of popular American literature, said this party experience and others convinced him that Tipton had a Peyton Place aspect under its disguise of boring conservatism.

(The Buddy Holly dance party Conn had attended memorialized the winter day in early 1959 when singers Buddy Holly, Richie Valens, and J.P. "The Big Bopper" Richardson, stopped in Tipton when their tour bus broke down. While it was being repaired the pop stars charmed the people they met. Four days later they died in a plane crash near Clear Lake, Iowa. For a few years this brush with the famous had been celebrated at a dance party at the local Moose club.)

◆   ◆   ◆

I met Bob Gelms on the last day of March, for an interview, oral history style, in the parlor of the Victorian mansion. He told a good story there, in an almost regal setting of handsome antiques, next to a polished green marble fireplace, a hand-painted flowery fresco overhead. Bob was a stocky man, 38 years old, round-faced with a trimmed red beard. He went to a Jesuit high school and considered becoming a priest. He was reserved in manner even though he had extensive disc jockey experience at brash and high-volume radio stations.

"I was born and raised in Chicago, and went to school either in the city itself or within a 60-mile radius. I was born and raised in the city proper, not one of the suburbs. A lot of folks say Chicago when they mean Oak Park or La Grange or something. I intended to teach college English and was in graduate school at the University of Illinois working on my master's degree when I was offered a teaching job at a college in Chicago and a radio job at a radio station. All this happened in three days.

"The radio job paid a lot more money. I thought to myself it might be a smart thing to do in the short run because I would always have the teaching thing to fall back on if I ever needed it. To this day I have never needed it. I have been in broadcasting since then. I took the radio job and finished up my M.A. (English/James Joyce) at the University of Chicago.

"I have always been on the air at any station I worked at, and off and on in management at various places. I lived in the fast lane in Chicago for nine years and there was only so much of that physically a body could take. I had almost reached the end of the road, I think, and I also was becoming quite dissatisfied with the kind of challenges that were presented to me and I wanted to do something else.

"I had been a writer for quite a long time and published a lot of non-fiction things in and around Chicago. Newspapers, magazines, almost entirely music related. Blues, jazz, rock 'n' roll. I've had quite a liking for blues ever since I grew up on the South Side. You would be walking down the street there and the music was coming out of a saloon. There's no way you could not be exposed to that on the South Side of Chicago, even to this day. I decided I was going to work toward a point where I would not necessarily be in broadcasting, at least as a full-time occupation. This was around 1981, '82, '83. By this time I was married to Chris.

"A lot of things happened in a very short time. We had had this house since 1979. At some point we were going to turn it into a bed and breakfast. I had been thinking more and more about doing that, renovating the house, thereby giving me an opportunity to develop an interest in writing fiction, which I had been unbelievably unsuccessful at. I have not published any fiction. Zero, nothing, zilch. I would dearly love to do that. That presents me with a great challenge inside myself. I know I can probably do it. I just need the time and treat it as if it is the bastard hobby of my life. I thought moving out here as a great chance to try.

"We began to have children. I began to think what it would be like for them to grow up in Chicago, in our condominium and not being able to go out at night. A few times we came out here and lived in this house for a week or two at a time. I really like the slowing down of the pace. I kept getting worried it might drive me nuts if I had to do it for a long time. A couple of weeks was great. But for a few years, I thought I might have problems."

I put my oar in and told Bob my brother Duane always said when you consider moving to a new address you should try hard to imagine what the place would be like at 4 p.m. on a Wednesday. Bob didn't say anything.

"I was working as an announcer at WLUP in Chicago. We made the decision to come here in 1984, in late spring or early summer. I worked on the house with Chris, doing renovation for six or seven months. At some point, it became obvious I needed to go back to work and earn some money. We had used up all the money we had. Luckily, my radio reputation from Chicago had preceded me and I didn't have a terribly difficult time finding a job in the Quad Cities. (Davenport and Bettendorf, Iowa, and Rock Island and Moline, Illinois.)

"In fact, I pretty much wrote my own ticket. This was in late summer or early fall of 1984. I was really particular what I wanted. I didn't want a full-time permanent job. I wanted a pretty good-paying part-time job that had an end to it. So, I did vacation shifts. That ended and I came back to work on the house. About a month later, the program director called me and offered me a job, and I said I don't want a full-time job. He thought I was holding out for more money and better conditions and I said, 'Look, Jim, I really don't want a full-time job. I came out here to do other things.' He asked me to work for him two to three months while he found somebody. I said fine.

"Halfway through we started getting bills from the plumber and the guy who did the roof and all of it was 50 to 60 percent higher than we had expected. The roof cost $4,500 not $2,000, and something else was $1,900 not $1,000. It became obvious I would have to go to work outside the house for a short time. The station I worked at was the kind of format I hadn't worked at for a long, long time, and I really enjoyed it. It was a CHR station, contemporary hits, loosely described as a Top 40 station. Disc jockeys talked before and after songs. They played jingles, lots of commercials, lots of personality. I liked the format. When it became obvious I liked it I went back to ask if the job was still open and it was, so that's when I went back full-time. I worked here too, maybe 20 hours a week.

"By early '86, the house was relatively finished and the business had started. Chris and I entered this whole thing making about every mistake. It has been a giant learning experience. We didn't plan in terms of finance. We were really naïve. We became serious students of the cost of renovation and labor. The place we opened in Bellevue, Iowa, (northeast of Tipton on the Mississippi) got done for less money and more work was done. We got very good at projecting.

"But with the radio thing, I started getting bored. I realized there was no place for me to go at that station. It was a radio station in the Quad Cities, not in Chicago. I was used a certain level of professionalism and that radio station did not come close."

Bob switched to another Quad Cities station, doing the morning slot, the "morning drive" shift on a grueling schedule.

"I never thought I would have the constitution to get up that early. I go to bed before my two-year-old kid does, about 8 p.m., and I am gone by a quarter after four in the morning. My show is from 5:30 until 9. Then I run the radio station until 2 or 3 in the afternoon. I'm the program director, with responsibility for everything on the air, hiring people, choosing the music. The station is brand new. It was a chance to start a radio station from the beginning. I know hundreds of people in broadcasting, and no one ever did that. And this is a 100,000-watt station, very powerful, the legal limit.

"It became difficult with this place because I was working full-time and then some at the station. When I eliminated myself from the picture here, it put quite a lot of pressure on Chris. It's been tough."

I asked him about Tipton, and how being a newcomer had worked out.

"The fact that Chris grew up here and knows a lot of people made it easier. But people still treat me standoffish. There are a couple of reasons for that. One, they don't know me, and number two, I'm pretty well known otherwise for what I do for a living. People might be a little intimidated by that. Also, we live in this house and people stand outside and look at this house and they might think, 'Yeah, he's on the radio in the biggest town around here, and they own this great house and another one in Bellevue.

"I know we have worked. This is the hardest I have ever worked in my life. The most difficult thing I have ever done. I have had to learn things that I thought I would never have to learn, and do things I disliked doing, like book work, and I don't do books real well. This idea of a bed and breakfast in the Midwest was a completely foreign idea, no one knew what it was. Some people thought we were starting a brothel. I'm serious."

The early morning drive to Davenport from Tipton took 30 to 40 minutes, about the same time as it took him to drive between his Chicago condo and his downtown job at the John Hancock Building. In Iowa, he was driving three times as far but using the same amount of time.

"I can't under any circumstances, and I mean that, think of a better place than Tipton to raise a family. I can think of about 500 places that are much better in terms of employment opportunities. You have to give something up to get whatever you want, to get a beautiful fine, nice, calm town with no crime. Here, everybody watches out for one another.

"To get that, you have to give up the chance and opportunity to make a lot of money like we were making in Chicago. What Chris and I did in a complicated and convoluted way was to convince ourselves this was going to work. We decided the only way we could sustain any kind of mental activity and not get bored or drive ourselves crazy from living in a town where there was nothing to do would be to work for ourselves. The way we saw to do it was to turn this place into a bed and breakfast, therefore attracting the kinds of people we really had liked and enjoyed in Chicago. They would come to us. It has happened.

"Some of the most interesting people I have ever talked to in my whole life I have met, sitting on this couch right here in this room. We don't have any television where the guests are, and no telephones or radios. There's a certain kind of person who approaches a bed and breakfast. They are a little more interesting and have traveled a bit and they are not afraid to talk to people and carry on a conversation."

I asked him how people in Tipton lived, from his perspective. "You are asking me a real interesting question. First of all, I don't spend an enormous amount of my free time outside of this house. I have never been a bar person, and one of the major occupations of men with free time is hanging out at the saloons. I know quite a few people, and some would like to get to know me better. And, I have got to know a few people, and they may talk to me about the stupid thing I said that morning on the radio. It's a way to start a conversation. I don't go out often. I go to Anderson's if I do. It's a younger crowd, with a pool table."

Bob's dad came occasionally from Chicago. Once, he went to Anderson's, got smashed and talked with great vigor to an old farmer about farming and hunting. "I am not good at that sort of thing," Bob said.

"We have close friends here, most of whom went away once and came back. One of Chris' best friends in the whole world is a lady who went to Cornell College (in Iowa), got a degree in German and went to Germany and met a Dane. Spent ten years there. Her folks died and left her the farm near Tipton and she came back to live there with her Danish husband."

I wondered how much he missed the Chicago job.

"It doesn't bother me working in Davenport after Chicago. If I squint my eyes and look at the Quad Cities, it looks a little like Chicago. It has a skyline, tall buildings, a river runs through the middle of it. There are four television stations, 18 radio stations, three newspapers. The people who live there look at it as seven different cities. The rating services see it as a metropolitan area."

I pressed him. Really? No regrets? No second thoughts about pulling out of the fast lane and moving to Hicksville?

"Not a one. I used to sail on Lake Michigan. That, I miss, a lot. I don't miss the money at all. I know that sounds ridiculous. The reason we moved here, and it sounds like one of those '60s catch phrases, but we wanted to improve the quality of our life, not necessarily the quantity. We had the quantity. Believe me. Chris ran a fur salon on Michigan Avenue and I was doing really well in broadcasting. We had a three-bedroom, 2,300 square foot condominium on the lake front.

"Famous folks. Springsteen, Mick Jagger, Ringo Starr, Paul McCartney. That never happens in the Quad Cities. I really, REALLY enjoyed these people. I don't want to sound jaded. I loved doing it. It was a neat experience to sit across the table from Mick Jagger and shoot the breeze with him for two hours. I saw the Rolling Stones five times. I saw Springsteen nine or ten times, and I would see him another nine or ten times. I've seen hundreds of bands, and once you have seen Cheap Tricks do their acts two or three times there was no sense going back. The only guy besides Springsteen I never got tired of was Muddy Waters. I saw him 20 or 30 times. He and I got to be pretty good friends. In fact, I produced his last album. I haven't gone to Chicago once since those days to see a concert."

Bob said if he quit his job at the radio station and could somehow replace the lost income, he could probably live in Tipton "pretty comfortably" because he knew a few people and being married to Chris had opened doors for him. "But a stranger coming to Tipton would have a very difficult time cracking any of those little cliques that exist here. But, another thing, a lot of people like us are coming back and we are developing into this little clique of outlaws or outriders."

"I do worry about Tipton's economic future. I think the way of life in small town America, small town rural America, has changed irreparably in the last 10 years because of the drastic effects of the farm economy. I have seen changes since I came here. Tipton never had a huge manufacturing base but the little amount it had has got up and walked away. Banks are regressive and narrow minded and they have to be that way because they have so much money tired up in bad loans in farmland.

"Starting a business that has nothing to do with agriculture is a difficult prospect because there is no loose money. A lot of businesses left because of that attitude."

After this song of mixed praise and despair, I wondered if he saw himself living in Tipton indefinitely.

"I could move tomorrow. It wouldn't pose any problems for me. I could stay for a while, too. There's a couple of places I would like to live before I get too set in my ways. Boston and Philadelphia. I do know I want to do this one other thing before I die. I want to live in a foreign country, as a foreigner. I want that experience. Maybe Ireland."

Bob ended the interview with a story. "A group of women came to the house, all of them 70 to 80 years old. I was talking to them about what it was like, and I mentioned as a newcomer to Tipton it was kind of difficult for me. One lady looked at me and shook her head and said I know exactly what you mean. I'm pretty new here in Tipton myself. I asked her when she moved here. She said 1936. She was not making a joke."

9

Bob was polite and careful, almost circumspect, about expressing his views about Tipton. He was a newcomer. Someone who was trying cautiously to find his way without calling too much attention to himself by being either too friendly or not friendly enough.

Christine's approach had a harder edge. She was well known for being outspoken. She was well known but not always well liked. Even though she had Cedar County pioneer ancestors, when she arrived in Tipton, a little girl without a father, she was a seven-year-old stranger with a Brooklyn accent and an irreverent sense of humor.

Unlike Bob, she was not mannerly. Tipton was "Snotpit," run by a "Main Street Mafia with a choke-hold on the town." Tipton was "a sliced white bread and mayonnaise society." Her negative feelings were intense but Tipton was home and at times she experienced heavy feelings of nostalgia and affection for the place she left with excitement and relief at age 18 and returned to with great hope and anticipation when she was 33.

She was good copy for Stu Clark. On an April morning he and I drove to the Victorian House in his little Dodge pickup so he could photograph a young woman steeplejack roofer working on the mansion's tower. Christine invited us in for coffee and cookies. We sat in her parlor for an hour and a half talking and joking. She was non-stop in the verbal department and had a jillion ideas on how to improve Tipton life. We talked about local scandals, and Christine unloaded amusing invective on merchants and bankers, the latter a group she considered, in general, to be "dick-less."

The 70-plus boss steeplejack, whose girl friend was hanging off the tower as we talked and drank coffee, told us about having illegitimate children with a Missouri woman. Later, I told Stuart the conversation and setting reminded me of Burt Lancaster and Deborah Kerr in the movie, *The Gypsy Moths*. The old womanizing steeplejack was like Lancaster in his unmistakable masculinity. Christine was in no way like the demure and somewhat sexually-repressed Deborah Kerr.

◆   ◆   ◆

Later that day, pursuing her constant search for antiques to install in her house or to sell, I went with Christine to the Phelps' place northeast of town where a farm house was about to be bulldozed. As Christine said, that was normal behavior for successful Iowa farmers. If something wasn't being used or couldn't be saved for spare parts or couldn't reproduce, get rid of it. She managed to hold off the wreckers long enough to scrounge for antiques in the house and nearby shed. After a fast search, she found a baby buggy, some old doors with fancy scroll work, a Victorian chest of drawers, a horsehair chair, as well as lightning rod cable and down spouts she could use at Victorian House. The men hauled a few well-worn horse collars out of a barn but she didn't want them.

◆   ◆   ◆

Christine was a hard interview. She had a jumping bean style, and was heavily hyperbolic. Her erratic talk ranged from unrelated anecdotes to one-liners delivered rapid-fire. After a while, I gave up and listened and laughed with her. I took notes and sometimes ran the tape recorder when she seemed to be on a steadier course than usual. One theme, though, threaded through most of what she said. She loved her old house.

She had grown up in a plain house next door to the imposing but crumbling Victorian on East Fourth Street. She was one of the few neighborhood kids, perhaps the only one, to develop a friendship with Ruby Wingert, the eccentric spinster who owned the mansion and lived in it alone. One of Christine's earliest dreams was to own Ruby's house. In 1979, before she married Bob and while living in Chicago working in a fur salon on Michigan Avenue, Christine did buy Ruby's mansion for $40,000. Ruby had been dead for 10 years and the tumble-down house was sold at auction. Christine bought it with a telephone bid. The word had been that the Wingert house would be torn down and the spacious lot with the old oak trees would be cut into little parcels for humdrum ranch-style houses. Christine couldn't live with that depressing possibility so she bought Ruby's old house.

After her homecoming and after she and Bob had restored the house and created a viable bed and breakfast business, Christine became known as one of the better cooks in eastern Iowa. She was described in newspapers as "chef Christine," a title that embarrassed her. She called her fare "Iowa gourmet," which to her mean simple food, fresh and well prepared.

◆   ◆   ◆

On a chilly April afternoon, we sat in the dining room and Christine talked and I tried to keep up. I had come with the intention of getting her life story in a fairly coherent narrative. She warmed up with a few stabs at Tipton.

"Tipton? It's future lies in its past. The apathy here drives me crazy. Remember Grant Wood's remark, "I had to go to Paris to appreciate Iowa?" I appreciate the real things here. They aren't invented or contrived, but Tipton is 20 years behind the times. In the '70s they were in the '50s. By now maybe they are 40 years behind."

I was curious about how Christine got to Tipton. She began the story with a history of her family, starting with her father's side. Her father's mother, Mary Zraick, was in on the founding of the firm that became Barbizon lingerie in New York City.

"A client list that included Du Ponts and the Biddles. Mary did everything for her kids. One went to Columbia, another to Harvard, a daughter to a finishing school in Europe. A tempered businesswoman, tempered by the motivation it was all for her children. A sweetheart, but a hard businesswoman.

"My father was Lebanese. He took electrical engineering at Columbia. His name was George Anthony Zraick. He was in the South Pacific during the war, mustered out as an officer. If he had stayed in, he would have ended up a general. My mother met him in San Francisco, probably in 1945, when my dad was bringing classified papers back, an intelligence assignment. My mother was just a dumb little shit from Tipton, Iowa. She had a civil service war job during the day and at night worked as an elevator operator in a downtown hotel. What she did, it was cute. She said my father got on her elevator and she took one look at him, and said to herself, 'He's it.' She paid all the other elevator operators not to stop on his floor. She continually stopped at the floor, figuring sooner or later he would have to get back on her elevator and she could meet him. He did. She did. They were married in two weeks!"

George Zraick was 13 years older than her mother. "My father was a handsome man, devastatingly handsome, so good looking he would be invited to many places simply because he attracted women."

◆   ◆   ◆

Her mother's maiden name was Long. Her mother's mother was a Carl, an old name in Cedar County. There are Carls buried in Rochester Cemetery, the county's oldest. The Carl tombstones are dated in the 1840s, about the time Iowa became a state. On one side of her family, Iowa pioneers, and on the other, Lebanese immigrants. Christine's last name, Zraick, in Lebanese meant "the blue," meaning royal blue. For some reason, she said, Iowans found the name hard to pronounce.

As a girl, after moving to Tipton from Brooklyn, Christine would be sent in the summer to stay with her grandmother in New York.

When the Tipton kid got off the plane at La Guardia, her grandmother would be waiting. She would kiss her, look at her and say something about new clothes. She came to New York looking like a kid from Tipton, Iowa; she went home looking like a kid from New York City. At times, she wasn't sure where she came from or where she belonged.

"I had two grandmothers without men. An American grandmother was left to raise a lot of children and make do. My father's mother was married to a Lebanese journalist who was killed. These women had to make do, without a man, when women were not supposed to do that. Maybe that is why I am so bullheaded."

She said her parents were very much in love. They had five children and lived happily and prosperously in Brooklyn. George ran electronics and TV shops. He had a cabin cruiser which they sailed on weekends. "Everyone said my father was an electronics genius. He had a string of repair and sales shops in Brooklyn, a good place to live back then. He called them Scott TV. He didn't want a Leb name."

Christine was born in 1950, on June 14, Flag Day. Early in life she had a case of the big head because on her birthday her father took her for walks in the neighborhood. He pointed to the flags and told his daughter they were flying for her on her birthday. Ever after, on June 14, Christine still half-believed him.

What she called a lovely childhood ended when her father died of lung cancer in 1957 at the age of 45. His widow was 32, with five kids and not a lot of money. She went back home to Tipton where her family lived. Mrs. Zraick met Ray, a printer at the Tipton newspaper, and married him. He loved and cared for her children as if they were his own. Christine called him "my dad," reserving "father" for George Zraick.

◆   ◆   ◆

In spite of her ambivalent attitude about modern Tipton, she loved to talk about her days at Tipton High. One of her favorite targets was the home ec teacher. "I hated cooking in high school. It was Gestapo cooking. "You must do it this vay! Hands on handles, not on wood! Tune in, girls!"

Christine thought it would be fun to make a papier-mache figure of the teacher, who was called "Gruny" behind her back, for art class. She used a Coke bottle as the main frame. "Gruny had the presence of an opera singer, a Brunhilde." Christine's art teacher also was not crazy about the home ec teacher, so he put the finished product in a prominent position in his class exhibit. The figure, which Christine had kept and brought out for me to admire, was amusing and expressive with its hair bun, turkey neck, outlandishly large breasts and protruding backside. The art teacher, saying it was true art and best thing Christine had ever done, gave it an A plus.

Her "Snotpit" nickname for Tipton, which did not set well with everybody who heard it, also came from high school. She was a cheerleader for the swimming team and while admiring herself in the mirror while wearing her TIPTON cheerleading sweater, realized all she had to do was an "s" at the end of mirror-image TIPTON to get SNOT-PIT.

Christine was graduated from Tipton High in 1968 and became an art student, briefly, at the University of Iowa. To help with expenses, she sold encyclopedias door to door, and was very good at it. She met Vince, the out-of-towner who supervised the local sales force. They were married before Christine finished her freshman year. For a few years after that, before their divorce, they led a wandering life. South Carolina, California, Colorado, Michigan, Indiana, Illinois.

After their divorce, Christine, with her wit and dark Lebanese good looks, was a social and business success in Chicago. She sold furs on Michigan Avenue and later ran two antique shops, while raising Caryn, her daughter with Vince. After half a dozen years in this fast life, she met Bob, an FM disc jockey, a semi-celebrity. They were married in 1980.

Shortly before that, Christine had bought the Victorian mansion in Tipton for a song, on a whim, really, and she didn't know what to do with it until the bed and breakfast brainstorm. In 1984, Christine and Bob and one-year-old Virginia, left Chicago for Tipton. Bridget was born in 1985 in Cedar Rapids.

◆   ◆   ◆

Christine's reasons for returning to Tipton were similar to Bob's. But she had personal reasons for being apprehensive. She was sensitive to the dangers of parochialism and isolation, especially concerning her children. She thought about these risks and arrived at a personal attitude she could live with. "I think as far as my kids are concerned, they will grow up feeling special, individualistic, in a small town. And, they have me. And, they can go to Iowa City for an education, and if they are lucky they will get a black roommate and somebody will hand them a funny cigarette. I think if small town kids are smart enough, and bright enough to keep their mouths shut, well, you can be the city sophisticate until they find out you are from Iowa. If you keep your mouth shut, people will take that for great intelligence. Like a farmer. Be laconic. If somebody graduates from Tipton High with the good education, and goes to college, they will do well because they have had the groundwork laid by fossils like Martha Jane Henry."

◆   ◆   ◆

Christine liked pithy sayings.
"God must have a sense of humor. He created Tipton, didn't he?"
"The guy's intelligent, that's enough to make you lonely in Tipton."
"The reason there are so few flies in Tipton is because most of the young men walk around with their mouths open."
"More pigs than people came out of Snotpit!"

"The Herbert Hoover Highway runs through Tipton. I think it should be renamed Highway to Hell."

◆   ◆   ◆

I walked back to my bunker as a yellow-green cloud in the west suddenly grew large. As I approached the courthouse the cloud let go with a deluge and hailstones the size of large marbles. I dashed to the shelter of the Hardacre's marquee. The storm lasted only a few minutes but left hailstones in drifts against the buildings. I figured spring was on the way.

The day ended with Conn at the Last Lap Tavern. Conn, although he enjoyed a lot of his work at the newspaper and liked a number of people in Tipton, admitted he was bored to tears, and lonely for "drugs, sex and rock 'n' roll." He was eager to be gone, into graduate school and the study of British social history.

10

Christine Gelms was not the only person to speak highly, even fondly, of the Tipton school system. Aside from hometown pride, Iowa was known as a state that took public education seriously. Iowans bragged their state had the highest literacy rate in the country.

I was curious about Tipton students and how they compared with those of earlier years. What happened to young people after they left Tipton High? Bill Diedrichsen was superintendent of schools. His office was in the three-story brick high school. Built in 1925, the building was immaculately clean inside and out and there were no rude slogans anywhere. Bicycles parked outside were not locked and there was no sign at the entrance warning all visitors to check in at the office.

Diedrichsen, in his mid-60s, was a quiet-spoken man with a sandy complexion. Born in Green Mountain in central Iowa, he worked for a number of years around Marshalltown as a farm hand, then as a carpenter, railroad worker, foundry worker. He served in the Army Air Force during World War II. Eight years after high school, he enrolled at Iowa State Teachers College (now the University of Northern Iowa). Diedrichsen decided to go to college but not because he was dissatisfied with factory work.

"I was doing great as a molder, on piece work. College, though, was something I hadn't done and I wanted to see if I could match wits." He was married to a school teacher, and she encouraged his interest in more education. Aside from that, Diedrichsen worried a little about silicosis if he stayed at the foundry. In 1951, he was graduated from the teachers college and came to Tipton as a biology and general science teacher. Three years later he was high school principal and became district superintendent in 1962.

"Students in the system now total 872. Our peak was 1,329 in the 1950s. There has been no change in the geographical area for decades. About two-thirds of the students come from the county area outside Tipton. The number from Tipton itself has declined but not as much as the county total. The physical size of Tipton has grown but the population is about the same. We used to run 13 school buses, 48 passengers each, now we run eight 54-passenger buses and they are not always filled. You don't have so many large families these days.

"The kids themselves since I came here, with television and all, I suppose they are somewhat more sophisticated but it is really a very good brand of people, if I can use that expression."

I asked him about discipline problems, drugs, the usual troubles.

"Through the '60s we had more problems with the real tough nut type. It never got out of control in any sense. Some people were really hard-nosed and difficult. That generation apparently had to go through this process. The Vietnam thing had some effect. Mostly, it was just plain defiance. If you told them, for instance, that they didn't belong in an area until the doors are opened, somebody would get defiant. Some drugs, some beer drinking, but early on we suspended some students. We didn't want to see how much we could punish them but we wanted to get them squared away. Sometimes we succeeded, and sometimes not. I am not naïve enough to say we have no drugs here now but relatively little, I think."

One thing I had noticed since I was accustomed to large cities was the lack of minorities. The last census said the county was 99.09 percent white, with .01 percent black, .23 percent American Indian, Eskimo or Aleut and the rest Asian or Spanish.

Earlier, when I talked to Herb Clark, the newspaper publisher, he couldn't understand where the minorities were living in Cedar County except, perhaps, for a few university people in West Branch. His conclusion was that since the census counts people in restaurants, a bus load of non-whites must have stopped at the Cove café and service station on I-80 at the same time the census counters arrived.

When I asked Diedrichsen about minorities in the schools, he said there weren't any. "In the past we have had some Vietnamese, and some Greek people who needed extra help in English. Way back in the history of this system we had some blacks. Unless you had several blacks enrolled, they would feel very much a minority here. Not very many black people went into agriculture, at least around here. We do have foreign exchange students every year. There would be enough prejudice here to cause some concern if we did have minorities. I have no doubts about that, especially among the older people."

Tipton has maintained a solid academic standing in recent years, he said, as high as it has ever been. "We do well on standardized tests, and rank high in Iowa, the 90th percentile, and Iowa does well nationally. We have the usual mix of slower learners and bright people, and the work ethic is not a great deal different than it ever was. Quality of our teachers is high. At least as many students go on to college, probably more than when I came. The student-teacher ratio is lowering. More special education. Our class size is closer to 20 or fewer, once it was between 25–30. We haven't reduced staff as fast as the student population has declined. You know, at times in the past, the students were hanging out the windows."

◆   ◆   ◆

Glenn Fear, 53, was the only counselor in the Tipton district, and the only full-time counselor the district had ever employed. He had graduated from Iowa State University and taught agriculture but became more interested in his students and their lives than he was in teaching agriculture. He got a master's in counseling at Iowa City in 1962 and went to work in Tipton.

I talked to him in his uncluttered, almost bare, office at the high school. Fear mentioned several important changes in society and in the students themselves since the '60s. "I think kids change gradually over time, sometimes so gradually it is difficult to see. For example, there was a period during the '60s when people were interested in doing what was best for society. They were very interested in ending injustice, now the pendulum has gone the other way, and it's more 'What's in it for me?' That's true in Tipton. I've had a lot of kids in 7th grade, that if you ask them what they want to do, and it's also true in high school, that the first thing they say is, 'I don't care, as long as I'm making all kinds of money.' A lot will say 'Win the lottery.' That's a definite change. And, it seems as if it were a fairly rapid change.

"Another is, when I came here, I could almost assume a student was living with both natural parents. Now, I have every conceivable combination. My primary counseling responsibility is grades 9 through 12, but increasingly I have gotten further into 7th and 8th, a few fireballs from 5th and 6th, and sometimes even younger.

"Two years ago I talked to more kids about suicide than I had in previous years. That was not something anyone ever talked about, or at least very rarely. But a couple of years ago we had a student who attempted suicide, and that opened the door to others who had thought about suicide. A few dragged a friend and told me, 'You've got to talk to her.'

"As I look back and remember the one who tried to kill herself, if you knew what I had known and had tried to guess who would try to commit suicide over the weekend, she would have been the last one you would have guessed. There were some factors, and unless you saw all of them, you wouldn't know. They were fragmented and she was the only one who knew them all together. She had gotten a bad grade, and she was not used to a bad grade. She got arrested for speeding, and something happened where she had worked. She took some pills and a fifth of wine."

I asked about drugs in general. "Drugs and alcohol are here. This is a very conservative area, so sometimes things are slow to reach here, or don't come in the magnitude they occur somewhere else. The local drug of choice is alcohol, but other things too, like cocaine and grass. No heroin that I know of. The vast majority of high school students have used alcohol. Alcohol has caused some problems, especially if they mix the drugs. I don't think the alcohol problem has changed much since I came here, maybe a higher percentage generally, and more girls drinking. I don't notice any distinctions between the town kids and farm kids when it comes to any of these problems."

Other patterns of life have changed, he said, especially family life. "A lot of kids have more money than they used to, with more freedom, and more mothers are working. More families are divorced." Fear estimated a 40 percent rate among his students' parents.

"One of my seventh grade sections had 13 kids, and I asked how many would sit down and eat one meal a day with their entire family. Two students raised their hand. That's a significant change. It's easy and handy for working mothers to make a plate for someone, leave it in the refrigerator, and the kid pops it in the micro. Mom's working a night shift, dad's working, the kid's working. They pass in the night, leaving notes on the refrigerator."

I asked him about minorities in the system. He recalled one black family, something like 15 years ago, with school age children but the family stayed only a year. He spoke of a girl, possibly of Hispanic background, who was adopted. Another was a boy, also adopted. "He's a little darker, but not Negroid."

"The gal is an attractive gal. I know she got hassled in middle school by a few, but not by anybody lately. They didn't know any better. Prejudice doesn't know any particular boundaries."

I asked Fear what happened to students after high school. "Most leave town, many to college. Anywhere from two-thirds to three-fourths leave town to get additional training, college or vocational school. Not a lot have entered the family business or stayed on the farm. They are certainly more mobile. A sizeable number went to Texas. With the oil boom petering out, some of those people are coming back. But the occupational opportunities here are dwindling."

Sometimes, he said, the ones who stay have a family business or farm, or have a feeling of obligation to family members who are ill.

"These people take a job, sometimes not a very good one, so they can stay. There are kids who want to stay around here, others wouldn't stay for any reason."

Fear seemed like a man content where he was. I asked him if he were. "Yes, I'm very happy here. Of course, I was born in central Iowa. I grew up on a farm west of Van Meter. I have been delighted to be here. I had had other opportunities, but I am still here and like it very much. We had three kids. The oldest is teaching deaf children in Texas. The middle girl is in her fourth year working in Tipton with retarded adults. Our son is going to Kirkwood (a nearby community college)."

Fear had no intention to leave Tipton eventually but said the decision would depend on where his children were when he retired. "We would like to get a motor home and wander. I'm married to a woman who is part Gypsy."

A few days later I ran into Fear at the post office. He had been thinking that morning while shaving and decided he wanted to emphasize a significant difference between now and twenty odd years ago. "People spend little time with their kids nowadays. Everyone has jobs. Maybe they have 15 minutes a day face to face, and this is spent mostly giving instructions. They may watch television together, but this is hardly important."

◆   ◆   ◆

Superintendent Diedrichsen had lent me a little book called "A History of Tipton Public Schools," published by the district in 1935. I was struck by some of the odds and end of information in it, none of which had any particular relevance to modern Tipton. I was intrigued, though, because these bits gave the town depth and a more poignant character than I had seen so far.

For instance, in 1895 a black high school student named Frank "Kenny" Holbrook was an athletic sensation. A stellar trackman, Holbrook also was a fine football player who made the team at Iowa during his freshman year, a feat few men had accomplished. At the time the book was published, he was the only black graduate of Tipton High.

Cedar County's renowned educator, Christopher Columbus Nestlerode, founder of the Tipton Union Free School in 1856, the first free high school west of the Mississippi River, received appropriate recognition. The book noted that Nestlerode, who was from Ohio, was considered a highly-educated man for his time. He had attended a common school and an academy. An eccentric, he once rode into town wearing a dressing gown, one shoe and one slipper. This behavior was described as "picturesque."

Also mentioned was Sue McNamara, an 1897 grad, an Associated Press correspondent who helped cover President Calvin Coolidge. A more interesting job for Ms. McNamara was being publicity agent for Miss Marion Davies, the mistress of William Randolph Hearst.

Of most interest to me was a speech by Charles J. Longley, who spoke at a memorial service in 1877 honoring the dead of the Civil War. It wasn't clear why this speech was detailed in the book, except that Mr. Longley devoted his talk to 24 Tipton men who did not survive the war. This speech has no particular connection with modern Tipton except that a tall white limestone Civil War monument to the Cedar County dead stands in front of the library. Mr. Longley's comments about the dead soldiers impressed me. They were sad and dignified, a piece of Tipton's history.

Some examples:

John C. Starr, 24th Iowa Infantry. "We left him beside the sluggish bayou and under the tropical verdure of the Pelican State."

J.E. Chrisman, 24th Iowa. "Starved to death in Andersonville's foul prison pen. A fate alike terrible and heroic."

James Edgar, 5th Iowa. "Shot to death in battle at Iuka, Mississippi."

James S. Carpenter, 24th Iowa. "Among the last of the sullenly retiring line at Champion Hill, on May 16, 1863, where he died, with his face to foe."

J.W. Dwigans, 11th Iowa. "Died of wounds received in the terrible battle of Shiloh."

George W. Simmons and Wilson Simmons, both of 11th Iowa. "Two brothers who died after the battle of Shiloh."

Carlos F. Weeks, 24th Iowa. "Shot to death in the battle of Cedar Creek, Virginia, and buried by the bright waters of the storied Shenandoah."

11

Along about mid-April, with its hints of spring, I quit tape-recorded interviewing. I had got about all I could asking questions during semi-formal sessions. I had a pretty fair cross-section. Some young, some old. Newcomers and old-timers. Professional talkers like newspaper editors, ministers, teachers. Farmers with pig shit on their boots.

Christine had joked about hiring me as a minimum wage handyman at Victorian House. I suggested she put me on the payroll at $4 an hour for a few hours a week. My life became a routine of Maid-Rite, bicycle to Victorian House, sometimes for a third or fourth cup of java before I started hauling garbage or chipping paint, lunch with Christine in her kitchen or with Conn or Stuart, usually at the M&L downtown. Later, I wrote letters and journal entries, and visited the library in the late afternoon or early evening.

Twice a week I drove to Iowa City where I observed a ritual of Hamburg Inn for a burger with everything, a chocolate shake and the *New York Times*. I spent time at the university library, maybe a beer at George's Buffet on Market Street before supper with my folks.

I cycled in the country around Tipton. By mid-April the weather was reasonable. During my rides west of town, I heard bird songs, sometimes a distant tractor. The farmland was alive, and the smell of freshly-plowed ground was a thrill that triggered boyhood memories of walking barefoot in a new furrow behind the plow and watching red-wing blackbirds eating grub worms.

A small sense of regret brushed me a few times as I watched the beginning commotion of spring plowing, fertilizing, farm equipment heading for the fields. I felt like a retired ball player who watched the game from the bleachers.

One warm afternoon, I sat in a white wicker chair on the porch at Victorian House with Christine and Bob. He was playing his guitar. I was looking at high-altitude vapor trails from transcontinental jets. Here we were on a spring day with the sound of blues guitar and playing children while the rest of the world hurried by. A bicyclist went past. The windshield farmer across the street was painting his Ford pickup's rear bumper. As Christine watched Ginny and Bridget pedaling their Big Wheels, she remembered Chicago. Gesturing toward her children, she said, "There's a big part of the reason we moved to Tipton." On the walk back to my bunker, Bob Jacobsen leaned out of his pickup with a wide smile and waved.

◆   ◆   ◆

Doc Esbeck invited me to go with him on an errand to South Amana, one of the old German villages west of Iowa City. A devoted woodworker, he had a pickup load of logs he wanted to drop off at a sawmill. Esbeck was laconic, in an easy-going way. When he did gab, he delivered some telling comments. He criticized farmers who over-cropped their land. He didn't miss a trick when it came to noticing cows about to calve. He said one sure way to cure farmland over-production was to take chemicals away from farmers. Chemical-free agriculture would bring people back to farming because the business once again would be labor intensive. He talked of old age, his dad's stroke, Alzheimer's disease and the joys of working with wood. He likely would retire before long but would stay in Tipton except for a bit of travel.

Earlier in the week at the Maid-Rite counter, Doc Esbeck had spoken of his four sons, all of whom, more or less, had stayed in the area. The current exception was his youngest who was a student at a college in Missouri. One taught sixth grade in Tipton, another was a carpenter in town, and the third worked at the steel mill in nearby Wilton Junction. Craig, the teacher, had been away for some years in New York and Denmark. The others, except for the student in Missouri, had never left.

◆   ◆   ◆

At the Maid-Rite a few days later, three guys wearing coveralls, jungle fatigue-style, came in for breakfast. They talked first about hunting wild turkey and crow and then, just as knowledgeably, about bicycling. In a nearby booth, three young men in white shirts and ties talked about financial planning. They were in money management. That morning the *Register* carried a story about a sociologist from the West Coast who said the Midwest, especially small towns in the Midwest, may be the next migration target because of open spaces, clean environment, crime-free society and the relatively low cost of living. I wondered.

◆   ◆   ◆

The Maid-Rite had become my hangout. For years, ever since getting into the habit when living in Honolulu, my greatest extravagance in daily life had been to go out to breakfast. The Maid-Rite was made to order. It was near my bunker and it was cheap. The hours were good. I depended on it, not as a place to go and talk to people. I was too anti-social and awkward to do that, but rather as a place to listen to conversations. By eavesdropping I was following an impulse that told me I would learn more by being a fly-on-the-wall than I would with big-mouth questions and a tape recorder. My feeling was that questions of the who, what, where, variety were not all that useful when it came to finding out how things were with people.

More than that, though, I simply looked forward to walking over to the café in the morning. It was a block away. I walked north up Lynn Street to the bean field, took a right and then another right up the alley behind the Maid-Rite. I usually bought a *Des Moines Register* for 35 cents out of the coin box at the Casey convenience store next door on Highway 38.

The Maid-Rite was a gray and white building with a half story below the ground, sort of a daylight basement effect. You stepped down to go in. Kay and Wally, the proprietors, lived upstairs. Capacity was 37, with booths, one table and an 11-seat L-shaped counter. The room was narrow and not long, maybe six paces by 12. No frills. A menu board was on the wall, pop and pie coolers at one end, a couple of fertilizer and seed corn calendars. No hanging plants or other gewgaws.

The café's popularity was amazing. People lined up when the place opened at 7 a.m. on Sundays and others, like Bob Jacobsen, were there at 5 a.m. the rest of the week. I think I learned more at the Maid-Rite than I did at any other place, and the food was cheap and good. A Maid-Rite hamburger was $1.30, a short stack and coffee, $1.51, mud and an English muffin, 87 cents. Coffee, a bottomless cup, was 50 cents.

Maid-Rite was an Iowa institution, with something like 100 franchises scattered from the Mississippi River to the Missouri. Maid-Rite, a trademark, means beef steamed loose. No frying and no patties. It's seasoned and put on a bun. Maid-Rite's first outlet opened in 1926 in Muscatine, a Mississippi River town. The philosophy: "Too good to be a patty." They are delicious. Each Maid-Rite is wrapped in greaseproof paper blazoned with the red and white Maid-Rite emblem and motto: MAID-RITE SINCE 1926.

People went there to meet their friends, others went to be seen so they might sell insurance or farm machinery. Lonely old people went for most of their meals and to break out of house-bound boredom. People dropped in after church in their best clothes, and sat next to dusty farmers in from the field for a quick bite before going back to the tractor.

Customers and waitresses talked and sometimes argued about pesticides, basketball games, Jesse Jackson and U.S. foreign policy. When they talked about blacks, the trigger usually was either Jesse Jackson, or college basketball and football players. The customers were not viciously racist. Some said nigger, others said black. In most cases, it was more like they were talking about something mysterious, from another world, a topic beyond their ken. Iowans, in fact, were fairly friendly to Jesse Jackson, probably because he seemed interested in their economic troubles. The Maid-Rite consensus was that Jackson would be a compassionate and decisive President.

At all times, customers were tuned into University of Iowa sports. To a lesser extent they talked about athletics at Iowa State University at Ames but the Hawkeyes in Iowa City were followed much more closely. There was very little interest in professional sports, although some did talk occasionally about the pros in Chicago.

Sports-related outbursts were not rare. One old man reading the *Register's* sports pages, almost became a stroke victim. "Stupidest thing I ever saw, and I've seen a lot!" he shouted from his seat at the counter. "Stupid, stupid, stupid! Iowa fouling Illinois trying to come from behind. Stupidest thing I EVER SAW and I've seen a lot of stupid things!" He sank back into the newspaper.

A few mornings later, an older than usual crowd was bellied up to the counter. A waitress brought up the possibility President Reagan would send troops to Honduras. Nobody supported the possibility. "That Reagan is a crooked bastard. He wouldn't know how to do anything legally, like declare war on somebody. Just look at his friends! Crooks!" said one man.

"Well," the waitress said, more bloodthirsty than her customers, "if they have to go, let them go to win, not just get killed."

If I had been a reporter on assignment to get man-in-the-street opinion on the issue of the moment, I would have been forced by journalism's code of objectivity to interfere with the flow of unvarnished opinions to identify myself as a reporter and take names. This move always wrecked the narrative, dried up free expression and often cleared a room. Instead, I smiled, drank more coffee, listened intently, grunted sometimes. Iowans are well mannered, usually, so nobody asked me what I thought.

◆   ◆   ◆

The Maid-Rite couldn't do it all. Often I remembered my discarded life on the Coast. In a springtime letter to my daughter in Seattle, I described my most serious problem of the emotional/nostalgic variety. In addition to missing her and a few friends, I was sorting out my feelings about the mythical West. I could not imagine not living there again. But when I tried to get specific about what I missed, except for people, I could think of only a few things—mostly places to eat breakfast.

For example, the Continental Pastry Shop (the Greek place) in Seattle's University District; the Beverly Hills Café at Wilshire and La Cienega; the wheat country in eastern Washington; Dorn's, a little café in Morro Bay where my 2nd ex and I ate breakfast many times; the beach at Stinson Beach, California, where my 1st ex and I had lived for a few months; the 25-mile stretch of I-5 between Yreka and Weed; the desert between Los Angeles and Las Vegas, maybe a couple of casinos in Reno; Highway 99, the eucalyptus and oleander route between Fresno and Bakersfield; the smell of mountain pine and desert sage. All these sensations could be filed under "cultural geography."

Otherwise, to be honest, I wrote Nellie that what I missed were places or sensations that didn't exist. San Francisco of the late '50s and early '60s; the orange blossom smell in Fresno in May; the old Fung Loy and Universal cafes in San Francisco's Chinatown; Ernies in North Beach which sold terrific combination sandwiches and sported great graffito in the men's room.

Another letter, to friends in Hawaii:

"I find I have some reservations about living in Iowa. I miss a sense of action, movement, even though I know that a lot of the action and movement is spurious and silly and contrived, based on Hollywood and TV dramas. I never liked the wet coastal Northwest much, and preferred the inland portion probably because the dry side reminded me of rural Iowa. Not the scenery. The people, the agricultural culture"

At times I was petulant. One afternoon on the way north toward U.S. 30, I was trying to get something listenable on the radio. WMT was reading recipes for MilkyWay sponge cake and every other available station was playing junk music or baseball. I blamed the lack of broadcast variety on the closed personalities of Iowans, admittedly a stretch of logic. Not free, not loose. Pinched. Christine liked to imitate Iowans by pursing her mouth tightly. Maybe, I thought, people were insecure from too much rural living. I thought of a bony old woman, skinny and lips pursed, who barely nodded when I said hello that morning as we passed on the sidewalk across from the square. She was wearing a silky black and gold IOWA jacket.

Going through an anti-rural stage, I wrote friends in Worcester, Massachusetts. In a letter, they got my goat by restating the old bromide about what a great place Worcester was for raising kids. Somehow, I equated Worcester with Tipton. "Your mention of Worcester being a great place to raise kids reminds me a lot of what people say here when I ask them why they choose to live in such isolation. Personally, I have always considered my rural Iowa rearing to have been a major drawback, a condition that set me back maybe 15 years in my personal development compared to people who grew up in New York or San Francisco or, even, Worcester. Norman Mailer wrote it was much better to have a guy from New York or Boston in the foxhole with you, rather than a farm kid, because the urban guy was quicker-witted and knew how to work with people. Of course, the farm kid may have been a better shot, like the bumpkin Sergeant York."

I think my April state of mind was expressed best in a letter to Quinn, a friend from Iowa City High School and the university. She lived in Amherst, Massachusetts. She and I went way back, long before she became an out lesbian and active feminist. We went as a couple to the City High Homecoming Dance in 1955, a big social win for me since Quinn, called Dorotha then, was one of the Homecoming Queen candidates. Her feminist revolt was far in the future. I recall that on that homecoming night both of us were scared to death she might be elected Homecoming Queen. That would make me Homecoming King and we would be forced to dance the first dance on the gym floor in view of practically the entire student body. She didn't win.

Her later rebellion against materialism and other aspects of ordinary life went deeper than my own. She had given up steady jobs for temporary ones, and moved around even more than I did. Everything she owned she could carry on her back. She was a deep thinker on social and political issues but she remained congenial to my fairly shallow personality. We kept in touch and I was very fond of her.

"You should be here tonight if you think Aprils in Amherst are cold. Mid-30s and a savage west wind. Coldest April in living memory I'm told but also the driest. So, it's an ill wind that blows no good. Of course, farmers would welcome rain. And bloody nearly everyone around here is a farmer, a retired farmer, or someone supported by farming. Except for the windshield ex-farmers who work in nearby "metro" areas.

"I have decided to let the Cedar County story unfold as it will. I am not killing myself with formal work. I have had enough of deadlines. Living is cheap and I can last a long time so I figure why worry? I can eat all the brown rice and black beans I want for pennies a serving.

"The Iowa life does not have me down for the count. I get exasperated at times with the slowness of things but realize it is false to complain too much since the slowness should not be news to me. Sometimes I think the people lack juice. I do think many people here exhibit what mental health workers call a flatness of affect but perhaps that is because the society is so homogeneous.

"My old Seattle newspaper life is dead and buried deep. Grass grows on the grave. My next undertaking of note is to march through my

long line of journals which I have accumulated here under one roof.
They go back to 1953. In a sense, I have holed up and intend to stay
until something tells me otherwise."

◆   ◆   ◆

Some of the best times were driving the 30 miles between Tipton
and Iowa City. One evening, at sunset on the road that goes north out
of West Branch and crosses the river at Cedar Bluff, I thought what I
needed for this Iowa time was a poet's sensibility, not the cynicism of a
burned-out reporter, a guy who doesn't want to work anymore or
think anymore or do anything but act like a daydream notion of a
western movie hero. I needed the talent of A.E. Housman and his
"blue remembered hills." I wasn't Housman so went back to looking at
the horizon.

The country at sunset was rounded like a naked woman lying on her
side, with only an occasional silo or barn or house to interrupt the sen-
sual line. The road dipped and climbed. I watched the country and listened to the engine and turned the country music louder. After
crossing the river I smelled thick moist new-plowed ground, musky in
a sexy way.

◆   ◆   ◆

I wrote Mike Dailey, an artist friend in Seattle who had grown up in
Des Moines. We met at the university in 1961 when he was more or
less a Commie, at least a hard core socialist, and I was a reporter for the
Daily Iowan. He and his wife Linda moved to Seattle after he got a
MFA and Mike taught art at the University of Washington and
became a well-known painter of abstract landscapes. Mike and Linda
were our landlords and neighbors when I was married and lived in the
University District. For years, I dropped in and Mike and I drank beer
or coffee in his studio and kitchen. We listened to country music and

talked about Iowa City during the salad years of youth and optimism. Urban renewal destroyed our old haunts of Kenney's and Ye Cozy taverns but we brought them back in memory with no difficulty.

When I told him I planned to return to Iowa and write about the experience, Mike said something that encouraged and inspired me. "In spite of all your changing places and moving around, to me, you have always remained an Iowan."

An April letter to Mike and Linda:

"I am reading the *Register* most days and clipping articles for my project. The paper ain't bad. I notice that my interest is mostly in "Iowa trends" news. Declining population, low birth rate, mass exodus of youth (nothing new there). I seldom read world news very carefully. It never changes anyway. Crises in the Mideast and Persian Gulf, Ireland, Detroit. Occasionally the paper runs a good series, especially ones on farming and demographic subjects. Iowa has the lowest birth rate in the nation, after West Virginia and Connecticut, and one of the highest rates of population decline, as well as one of the oldest populations. By 2010 at present rates it will be about where it was in 1900, 2.4 million. (Note: This forecast was wrong. Iowa lost population between 1980 and 1990 but was back to more than 2.9 million in 2000, slightly above the 1980 figure.) In 1987, the birthrate, 13.2 per 1,000, was the lowest it had been since the state began keeping records. Housing is disappearing with a net decline of 16,000 units since 1980. Business people worry about finding enough workers, skilled or unskilled. I suppose these problems are not all bad if you don't mind being lonely for variety in people and culture, if you have strong inner resources and maybe an income independent from economic realities.

"This morning I saw a bumper sticker on a Chevy pickup parked in front of the Maid-Rite. Too old to work, too young to die, so bye-bye. Most mornings I hit the Maid-Rite for a short stack and mud, read the paper and listen to conversations. Mornin' Ed, how're ya doin'? Got any corn in yet? Well, at least the wind ain't blowin' yet. Shoot, I thought it would never quit."

"I have given up on any coherent approach to life here. I now consider myself a romantic T.E. Lawrence personality who has been in the middle of something elsewhere and has come to a place to hide out to pursue private matters. My handyman job is kind of like Lawrence's life as Aircraftman Shaw, an obscure gentleman ranker who rode a motorcycle around the countryside until the cycle killed him. I ride a bicycle, which is safer as long as you don't ride at night."

◆   ◆   ◆

On a Friday night at the end of April, Conn Meade and I went beer-drinking at Tipton's downtown trio of taverns. Conn was leaving for Dublin the next week. Already I was missing him. He wasn't worried about much that night, and at the North Star Lounge he said he could not wait to get back to a city and the bars, the cafes, the women, even the buses. Conn was even a bit nostalgic, unusual for him. He talked of his dad's friends of years ago, some of them old time IRA hard men. Cold eyes. And always guns when they came to call.

12

I liked cemeteries. I liked wandering in them. They were full of stories. My dad had been, among other things, a grave digger and cemetery sexton. When he was in the digging end of the funeral business in the 1950s I helped during the summer and any other time he needed a hand. As a high school and college student I mowed cemeteries for a summer job. I liked the quiet and dignified atmosphere.

When I lived in Tipton I kept up my cemetery interest, and in Cedar County I occasionally saw a name I recognized on a tombstone. Eventually I ran into Ruby Wingert who apparently, I found out later, divided her time between her official address at the Tipton cemetery and her former address at Victorian House.

An old, maybe the oldest, graveyard in Cedar County was Rochester Cemetery south of Tipton, also known for its native prairie flowers and grasses. On its west side, in the winter when trees are bare, there is a commanding view of the Cedar River and the country beyond. I often visited in the early evening to watch the sun go down behind the river, tall gravestones standing in silhouette.

Francis M. Baker was buried at Rochester, and I always stopped by at his grave when I visited the cemetery. Mr. Baker, born in 1864, died in 1945, not long after he had lived with us for a while at the Cedar County farm, a farm where he had lived for many years. He had sold the farm before we moved in but stayed with us for a few weeks afterward, apparently because he wasn't ready to leave the place where he had lived for so long. He was a nice old man in his 80s who loved my mother's french toast. Mr. Baker moved across the road to live out the rest of his life with his son, Clarence. The old man died one morning either on his way to or from the outdoor toilet.

Clarence's wife, Nettie, shouted across the road to my dad who was working in our barnyard. "Lysle! Come quick. Something has happened to Frank."

Clarence and Nettie were the ideal farm neighbors. Always available to help, friendly people with no pretensions, they became close friends with my parents and the friendship lasted until Clarence and Nettie died. Clarence and Nettie farmed 80 acres, raised a family and made a good living, an indicator of how things had changed between '45 and '88 in the business of farming. He was known throughout the area as a first-class farmer, and often was identified as an "AC" man or a "Chester White man," because he farmed with Allis-Chalmers equipment and raised Chester White hogs. I remember the day a few years after the war when Clarence traded his brown '38 Chevrolet in on a new Chrysler New Yorker. You couldn't get more successful than that.

During my cemetery visits, usually while bicycling, I looked for pithy epitaphs. My favorite overall was one that came from literature: "Young, she entered the portals of dust" (Edgar Lee Masters' *Spoon River Anthology*). My Cedar County favorite was engraved on a white stone at a tiny almost-forgotten cemetery west of Tipton.

ROBERT MCNAIR
DIED
JUNE 14, 1860
AGED 54 YEARS
4 MS & 11 DS
HE WAS TOO GOOD TO LIVE ON EARTH
YET TOO YOUNG TO DIE

◆   ◆   ◆

One grave I visited frequently at Tipton's main cemetery, called the Masonic, had no epitaph, only a simple flat granite marker.

RUBY E. WINGERT
1887–1969

Ruby, the maiden lady resident and owner of the Victorian mansion, had been young Christine Gelms' next-door neighbor, a woman feared as a witch by neighborhood children, a near-recluse in her old age. Miss Wingert was buried in her family plot in the big cemetery on the west side of town past the country club on the road to Cedar Valley. She was next to a brother, "Little Foster," who died in 1888, aged four days. Next in line was John B., who died in 1887, aged four years, seven months, sixteen days.

Miss Wingert lived in the mansion at 508 East Fourth Street most of her 82 years. The last months at the end of her life were spent in a Tipton nursing home. Her parents, banker and landowner Frank Wingert and his wife, Emma, bought the house in 1898 for $15,000. The Wingerts moved into a house then considered one of the show places of the town. One of three daughters, Ruby grew up to be a slim and aristocratic young woman, rather horsey in the face.

The house, designed by New York architect S. B. Reed, was built in 1883 by John C. Reichert, a lumberyard owner who wanted to show off his wealth. Victorian architecture was an excellent vehicle for ostentation because the style has been characterized as "too much is just enough" and "excess is just right." The mansion, with a full basement, three full floors and an impressive tower, was "stick Eastlake" in style. That meant an angular, tall wooden structure, imposing in an upward, soaring way, with embellishments of gingerbread millwork. The roof was slate, and inside were two Vermont marble fireplaces, hand-painted frescoes on walls and ceilings, a magnificent main staircase. The general effect of the house, inside and out, was well-built and spacious luxury.

The original interior decorator was a man named Will G. Andrews, who spent two years on the job. On the third floor landing the craftsman had signed his name and dated it before applying the last strip of wallpaper. When the Gelms uncovered it during renovation, they saw:

"Will G. Andrews, fresco painter and decorator, Clinton, Iowa, April 6, 1885.

The original owner installed indoor plumbing which included a third-floor 925-gallon copper tank fed by rainwater. Each room had stained glass windows of the same colors as the original paint scheme. When the Wingerts moved in, they added electricity and new carpeting on the formal stairway but left the Belgian rugs in the formal parlor, the music room and the dining room.

As the family died off or moved out, Ruby stayed. She was a frightening figure to children. She wore odd clothes and had funny ways. Christine visited one day and Ruby told her, "I have a dog, you know." Ruby showed Christine her beloved Buddy, dead for years, but preserved very well by the wonders of taxidermy. "I had a brother too, you know," Ruby said. Christine was terrified, and expected to see a well-preserved long dead brother.

Christine loved Ruby stories, although some perhaps were in the category of legend. Ruby was said to have raised chickens upstairs, and was known around town as a person who took fresh flowers off graves and used them in garden club competition. She won prizes at the county fair, and one year won first prize for canned gooseberries. Next year she went back and won a red ribbon even though a judge suspected it was the same jar as the previous year. When she returned a third time with gooseberries, a suspicious judge opened the jar. Ruby had added formaldehyde as a preservative.

Ruby was rumored to have asked a hostess at a large luncheon if she could have the leftover lettuce to feed her rabbits who lived in a jungle-like thicket at the rear of her property. Instead of feeding the rabbits she apparently served the lettuce at one of her own luncheons.

◆   ◆   ◆

These stories were ancient history. The ghost stories were not, and dated from the Gelms' takeover. One evening at dinner in the dining room next to the kitchen, after Christine had told some Ruby stories, a dinner plate suddenly and loudly cracked. Another time, Christine told guests how Ruby had caught a bat in a jar. One of the women guests became upset, saying she was deathly afraid of bats. Christine assured her that they had never seen any bats in the house.

That night, late, the woman who was afraid of bats started screaming. Bob and Christine raced upstairs and the woman told them she had seen a bat in her third-floor room. After the crisis was over, they came back to their second-floor bedroom to find three-year-old Ginny in their room, awakened by the ruckus.

"Who was the lady in white sitting on your bed?" she asked. Ginny said the lady was rocking back and forth and laughing while people ran around upstairs chasing the bat. After all was quiet the lady in white floated to the ceiling and vanished.

Another time, two guests came in after a walk and asked about the pleasant old woman they had met on the sidewalk near the house. She told them she lived in the mansion. She had a white dog that looked a lot like Buddy.

Later, two honeymooners asked one morning about the lady wearing bright red lipstick who told them she lived upstairs. They had met her coming out of the third floor bathroom. No older woman lived upstairs, Christine said, although a lady named Ruby Wingert, who had been dead since 1969, had lived in the house and was partial to bright red lipstick.

Deidre, an assistant innkeeper at Victorian House toward the end of my stay in Tipton, told me another story about Ruby, unprompted by Christine.

"I saw her," said Deidre in a matter-of-fact way.

Two weeks before our conversation Deidre had gone after dark to the second floor stairway landing to unplug Christmas lights. She leaned over to pull a plug and felt a tingle as if the hair on the back of her neck were standing on end. She looked downstairs. A short woman in a long, beige dress was standing in the dining room doorway. "She was in 3-D color. Nothing white. She had a long, horsey face. She reminded me of my dead grandmother."

Deidre blinked, she said, and looked again. The woman smiled and nodded her head. "It was Ruby. I ran to the bedroom and tried to tell Lee what I had seen. I couldn't speak."

On other nights she and Lee, her husband, had heard footsteps in the room directly above their bedroom. The upper room had been Ruby's playroom as a girl. The footsteps were heard on nights when no one was staying upstairs.

I got to the point where I half-believed these stories. When I lived in St. Ives, in Cornwall, England, ghost stories abounded in the spooky environment of the moors and Iron Age artifacts. In Cornwall, I had a few ghostly experiences myself. Finally I decided if there were ghosts they had been there long before I arrived and would be there long after I was gone.

In Tipton, I fairly frequently bicycled to the Masonic Cemetery to sit awhile at Ruby's grave and talk to her. A monologue, but satisfying. I told her ordinary things, such as how business was going at Victorian House, that I was painting the front steps and porch railing, that the roof had been repaired and we were cleaning some of the basement rooms. When I drove by the cemetery on my way to or from Iowa City, I was in the habit of looking toward her grave and honking and yelling out the window, "Good night, Ruby. Sweet dreams."

13

May was the big push for farmers. I wasn't a farmer so I decided to make my May push at the Maid-Rite and Victorian House. I drank Maid-Rite coffee, ate English muffins and read the *Register*, at a semi-retired pace, followed by mowing, raking, hauling, scraping, painting, planting, eating lunch and enjoying coffee breaks with the Victorian House honcho at the kitchen table.

Aside from lunches and coffee breaks, a typical work day at the mansion lasted two or three hours. In the early summer, before I ran over a large rock and busted the lawn mower, the major job was the mammoth yard. After the rock incident, the Gelms hired the yard work done professionally. Scraping and sanding and painting the wrap-around front porch became an interminable job which I never finished. I enjoyed the work although it was hard for a middle-aged layabout to do that much physical work without feeling it.

I picked up a new appreciation for the value of money, and realized how well I was paid at the newspaper for doing very little or almost nothing for days on end. By working hard for a few hours a day at Victorian House, I was able to pay my outlandishly low rent, buy some grub, some beer and pay for postage stamps. This part was good but I soon realized some things were too expensive for my present income. The bicycle I rode to the mansion in the morning would cost about $500 new, which represented a lot of scraping and painting. The shoes I wore represented 10 hours of low-wage work. Going to lunch was the same as working an hour or more. It had been a long time since I thought of money in real terms.

Early in the month, while wolfing a terrific lunch of roast chicken, rice and peas, Christine's heavenly walnut-laden cole slaw, corn, and fruit salad, I chatted with Elva, Christine's new kitchen helper. Elva talked about her wages ($3.40 an hour) at a local factory, where her job was to help manufacture a small electrical component for automatic garage door openers. She said the highest hourly wage for labor was $4.50, and one worker making $4 had left recently after 13 years. Elva quit, even though she had two kids and no husband. The dad was somewhere in Oregon.

Another Victorian House worker was Al, a sophomore at Snotpit High, who had been working at one of the local pizza emporiums for $2.50 an hour washing dishes six hours a day. Some of the people at the pizza place didn't speak fluent English, and often Al couldn't understand a word they said. He appreciated working at V.H. because it was an English-speaking environment and he was earning $1 an hour more. Al was a likeable kid, who dressed in black like his idol Johnny Cash. I pumped him for real-life Tipton lore from the teenage perspective.

For entertainment, Al said, the locals went to Iowa City or the Quad Cities to hang out at teenage night clubs. Al admitted they often got into fights due to a kind of gang mentality. He doubted a teen joint would make a go of it in Tipton because the kids wanted more than anything to get out of town at least one night a week. He lived on Snaggy Ridge along the river north of Rochester. He drove an old International pickup which he loved, apparently more than anything in the world.

A kitchen colleague, a half-Filipino boy, was less friendly toward his environment. He disliked Tipton and said he could not wait to be graduated from high school so he could move to San Diego. His judgment: "Tipton is too slow, too many chicken shit conformists."

After the gourmet lunch, I put in three hours helping in the yard, planting flowers, trimming trees, hauling grass cuttings. The most disagreeable task was cleaning Pierre Lapin's cage. This extra-large brown rabbit was a house favorite and bounded about inside unhindered most of the time. A sometimes vicious beast, he was tolerated and even pampered. For $4 an hour, such a deal for the Gelms, I was yardman, garbage hauler and rabbit shit house cleaner.

I continued to marvel at how hard it would be to make $4 an hour and live halfway decently. I looked at my shoes again. A 12-pack of beer was $5. Enough stamps and postcards for a bit of correspondence cost an hour's pay, the utility bill for March was a full day's pay. An evening meal and a night's stay at the V.H. would be about two day's pay, and if you brought a woman it would run you about a week's pay. And so it goes. No wonder people working at the bottom of the pay scale sometimes think either of making a buck illegally or dropping out altogether.

On the plus side, I enjoyed the work, more than I did the last year dealing with mean-spirited editors. Of course, dealing with mean-spirited editors earned enough money to be tolerant of a short-term low-wage job. When I finished a job at V.H., I could tell myself the yard looks really nice or those steps look fine. In a few weeks I could say I planted those flowers that are blooming so prettily over there by the oak tree. One day Christine and I planted flowers in a circular plot, and later we put in four little evergreens along the driveway. When we were through planting the trees, I looked at them and knew the trees would be in Tipton long after I was gone.

◆   ◆   ◆

Sometimes during lunch time at the mansion, I played court jester while Christine and her helpers worked on big luncheon contracts. I told the women I had dropped out after making my wad and the $4 an hour at Victorian House paid my incidental expenses and, in addition, I liked the company. I described myself as semi-retired, a man of literary sensibilities too good for the daily newspaper world. The helpers always laughed, and often joined me in clowning antics, the same adolescent behavior that got me in trouble during my days as a reporter.

This behavior did not always amuse Christine who had to pay the bills, fight off creditors, get the business in and then work to keep the business coming back. The place often was almost impossible. Telephone service was cut off for lack of payment. Ginny and Bridget threw tantrums at critical moments. Kitchen help decided to quit because the work was too hard, the boss too demanding or too obnoxious. Christine had bitter disputes with the linen service man. Law suits were threatened for one thing or another.

In the midst of chaos one morning, Christine almost fainted when the city health office called and said it was time for a kitchen inspection. She recovered when told not to sweat it. They wouldn't be out that day and would let her know when they would be. Through all the pressure, Christine carried on, in spite of her temper outbursts, cascading money problems, labor troubles. In the dining room where the guests ate off white linen with antique silver, all was genteel and calm, while in the kitchen the scene was fire, flood, hail and tornado.

Christine's secretary Marcie, a middle-aged woman with a reservoir of Midwestern common sense, kept the business in order. She kept a firm hand on the tiller and maintained a position above the trivia of emergencies.

◆   ◆   ◆

The girls, Ginny and Bridget, were a hair-tearing trial to everybody at times. They fought, screamed, demanded favors, spilled food and drink. I liked them immensely, a reaction that baffled me since I usually avoided children. The girls were interesting specimens because both were foxy and pretty and articulate. They mirrored their parents in a sort of reverse way. Ginny, five years old, fairly quiet most of the time, was dark and black-eyed, smart in an academic and questioning way, like her dad. She looked nothing like him. She had her mother's Mediterranean looks. Bridget, barely three, was fair with reddish hair and sparkling eyes. Her face was round, happy and expressive, although not as striking as her sister's. Bridget was evanescent, capricious in her moods, a charmer, especially of men. She was like her mother but her looks came from her father. No one would have guessed she was Christine's daughter on looks alone.

One night, gazing at a full moon, the girls indicated perfectly their different attitudes. Ginny turned to me and said: "The moon, it's made of dust and rocks, isn't it?"

Bridget heard her and said firmly, "No, Ginny. The moon is made of ponies and ribbons."

◆   ◆   ◆

At the Maid-Rite I read a big spread in the *Register* about crowding troubles on both coasts. Proof, said the paper in an editorial, that life in Iowa was not as hopeless and dismal as resident complainers thought. The Iowa birth rate was low and the population was aging rapidly. The *Register* noted, though, that in Iowa you could breath the air without fear, time in traffic was negligible and people who weren't millionaires could buy property.

The same day, relaxing at an Italian café in Iowa City with Conn and Christine, I thought of the *Register's* comments. In a warm mood, I decided I agreed. Iowa was not a bad place, all my whining and moaning aside. We were having an excellent Italian-style country lunch, drinking fine old-fashioned beer from Wisconsin. A touch of European culture, edible pasta, drinkable regional beer, witty conversation, a warm spring day, all giving an edge to life. What more could I reasonably ask for? One drawback. I was in Iowa City, not Tipton.

Christine brought up her latest dream. She wanted to start a sandwich shop in downtown Tipton. Conn, cynical and realistic, said he didn't think the M&L courthouse crowd would ever break the habit of walking across the street to the M&L no matter how wonderful C's eatery might be.

It was our last day with Conn. He was to leave the next morning for Dublin. A memorable day. Conn was wearing black jeans and a dark jeans jacket, a black cap and dark opaque sunglasses. With his gaunt look and self-confident manner, he reminded me of the Rolling Stones. Christine had on a long dress with a sash, and looked exotic, perhaps a bit Ruby-esque/eccentric in a costume topped by a floppy straw hat. I wore my brown Eddie Bauer bush hat, along with my usual khakis and blue work shirt. When we got back to the mansion all mellow from Wisconsin beer and Iowa City ambience, Bob was home and annoyed with us. We had been enjoying the best Iowa had to offer while he was shouting into a microphone doing his Quad Squad number.

◆   ◆   ◆

I needed a break from domesticity. A lot about V.H. I liked. The work, the boss, the kids, the lunches, the help. But it was planting time in Iowa. I took a day off to see for myself a different way of farming, one that would eliminate a prized Iowa memory. The plowed earth smell, for me, was a main reason for being in Iowa in the spring. You didn't smell it as much anymore. That's because some farmers were doing something different, a new way of farming called "no till," which meant no cultivation.

Larry Glick was a leader of the no till movement. I drove west of Tipton across the Cedar to talk to him. No till meant no plowing or disking or harrowing, which all had been critical to my spring memories of black and fragrant soil. With no till, a farmer simply pulled into a field of harvested corn or beans and planted again by using a special planter which cut through the stubble of last year's crop, bypassing all the old preliminary steps of preparing the soil.

No till fields look bad, "junky," full of stubble and debris from the previous crop, with the same appearance before and after planting until the new crop appears. Under the traditional method of cultivation, newly-planted fields looked clean and neat, geometric in their orderliness. All stubble was sliced and plowed under. No till supposedly reduces erosion and holds moisture better, along with savings associated with using less equipment, fuel and time. Critics said no till required farmers to use more chemicals to control weeds and pests but Glick said that had not been his experience.

◆   ◆   ◆

No till was interesting to me because of its vast difference to the way my dad, with my immature help, did field work in the 1940s. After disking, then plowing, followed by harrowing, we used a McCormick-Deering two-row corn and soybean planter so old it originally was designed to be pulled by horses. This antique even had an iron seat where the original operator had sat holding reins for a team of horses.

When my dad and I planted corn or beans I rode on the planter's iron seat while he drove the tractor. My job was to watch for malfunctions such as dirt clogging the planter or seeds failing to drop in the shallow furrow made by the planter's "shoes." I also was supposed to check that the little seed furrows were covered properly by the planter's grooved wheels. At the end of each run across the field, I heaved back on the lever that regulated the depth of the shoes and hence seed depth. This action of raising the shoes stopped the mechanism. My dad turned at the end of the row, realigned the tractor and planter for another run across the field. I released the lever, the planting mechanism resumed proper depth and the process resumed. When I remember planting I hear the busy clicking of the mechanism, the throaty rumble of the F-20 Farmall, and I see my dad's broad back a few feet ahead of me on the tractor seat.

We didn't use chemicals and I don't recall anyone who did. We did mix something black with the seed soy beans but I think this material was nitrogen to give a boost to the beans. No sprays or powdery insecticides or herbicides. As a result we spent a lot of time in mid-summer pulling button weeds out of the beans, pulling morning glories off corn stalks and chopping Canadian thistles.

Weed control in the corn fields was mainly a piece of equipment called a cultivator which was mounted on the tractor and uprooted weeds between the corn rows. This method of controlling weeds ended when the corn was as tall as the tractor's axles. After that the corn was on its own.

◆   ◆   ◆

Glick was working in an unplanted corn field on his place a mile west of Cedar Bluff on the road to West Branch. I talked to Glick, 42, college educated and sporting a red beard, as he loaded his $12,000 six-row planter with seed corn, insecticide and fertilizer chemicals. He loaded the insecticide boxes on the planter with a dry chemical called "Counter." He poured fungicide-treated seed corn into the seed boxes. Lots of chemicals and lots of warnings on the bags not to breath it, eat it, or even smell it for long. His tractor was huge, a White, the Field Boss model, a product of a merger between Oliver and Minneapolis-Moline, two off-brand tractors of my day.

No till, said Glick, had been good to him. He and his dad, who was 79, raised corn, beans and cattle on 900 acres and they tried to do it without hiring any more help than absolutely necessary. No till cut down remarkably on field time because there was no preparation. Last year they harvested 172 bushels of corn per acre off one of his no till fields, an above average yield for them.

After listening to him extol the strengths of no till and watching his crisp movements with the fertilizer and the seed corn, I didn't mention how much I missed the musky smell of freshly-plowed ground. I thought the sentiment would make me seem about as outdated and backward as our old two-row museum-quality McCormick-Deering planter. Glick mounted his Field Boss, hydraulically lowered the $12,000 no till planter and was gone, crashing through last year's stubble. I watched this field grow to maturity and the corn looked good even during the worst of the summer drought.

◆   ◆   ◆

That evening I dropped in on Bob Jacobsen in his office at Edler Implement-Massey Ferguson. He was busy as a cat on a hot tin roof. Spring and fall, the planting and harvesting seasons, were his busy times. He had time to tell me that the previous year he grossed a million dollars but finished with a net profit of $20,000. Money had become a bit looser but he still wasn't selling many big ticket new machines, tractors and combines. He sold maybe four big new tractors a year. He was selling more used machinery, and lately quite a few new manure spreaders because livestock growers had some money for the first time in years. He bought the implement business in 1985, at the bottom of the farm depression. And so he got a fairly good deal on the price. Times were better, although people in the business were wary and often asked for cash on the barrel head instead of giving credit.

◆   ◆   ◆

I didn't talk to a lot of farmers about their business but my morning with Glick indicated again, as I had found in other conversations, that farmers seemed to be basically optimistic about farming in Iowa. Men I did talk to were family farmers and in nearly every case their family had been on the same land for two or more generations. They had a good base of farmland, often paid for, and a strong background of experience. If asked about the wisdom of coming into farming cold, with no base of paid-up land and a comfortable amount of working capital, they would grin and shake their heads.

An old friend, Dick Oberman, a man I had gone to high school with, ran a corn, soybean and hog operation southeast of Iowa City in Johnson County. He was in with his dad and, with a hired man, they worked 760 acres, with about a third in conservation reserve. The remainder was about 50-50 corn and beans. They raised some 2,000 hogs a year. In 1958, they started with 160 acres, and added the rest over the years, most of it at fairly reasonable prices. During the boom, however, when the government was advising farmers to plant fence row to fence row and beans were going for $12 a bushel, the Obermans bought 80 acres for $2,800 an acre. This land was overpriced, in the perfect hindsight of six years later. Dick was fully mechanized, including a $106,000 combine for corn and bean harvesting.

In spite of hard times, Dick told me "the sky's the limit in family farming if you follow good management techniques." Iowans should not be afraid of bigness in agriculture, he said, and emphasized that "farming is not a way of life, but a business," and he insisted that is the only way to look at the subject.

He felt much of the farm problem was based on poor management, over-extension of investment, sometimes simple greed. But he acknowledged he and his dad made some lucky buys of land before inflation struck. They owed a good deal of money but the debt was "manageable," a key word in his farming philosophy. His fondest hope was that his son, 24, working at a hog factory in North Carolina, eventually would come home and work on the family farm.

◆   ◆   ◆

On a morning in May, I walked to the Maid-Rite and listened to the sort of conversation I called "Good Maid-Rite."

A customer at the counter said: "A great morning, isn't it?" He took a deep breath of the air coming in the open window behind him.

A man from town replied: "All I smell this morning is farm chemicals." He railed against chemicals, citing a recent experience of seeing a farmer using a spray rig which was set so high the wind blew most of the spray back into the road. "More spray went on my truck than on the field," he said.

These comments triggered a response from farmers in nearby booths, mostly to the effect that the offending farmer had set his boom too high. It was too windy. He was using the wrong nozzles. Technical clarifications.

"I suppose so, maybe," said the man from town, "but this morning all I smell on the wind are ag chemicals." Frowning, he paid his bill and left.

One of the farmers kept the topic alive by saying he had spent the last three days getting a license to spray on his place, but he constantly saw people in town ineptly spraying 2-4-D and fertilizer in their huge yards, filling the air with chemicals. "Why don't they need a license?" His fellow farmers grunted in agreement.

Pesticide and herbicide conversations were more argumentative than most. On another occasion, the anti-chemical waitress braced an old farmer by announcing, as he quietly settled into his coffee and sweet roll: "I wish you guys would stop putting all that chemical on the soil, that's what I wish."

His reply was the same as it always was in these conversations, kind of resigned and tired, even sad. "I wish we could too, but what are we supposed to do? We don't have a choice if we want to survive. Most years, we wouldn't have much of a crop without these chemicals."

The talk normally was centered on safer topics, like pickups, with the traditional division between Ford and Chevy owners. "A man who owns a Ford is a poor man," said one man, with his buddy replying he had owned Fords all his life and liked them a lot. "Always had good luck with them." There was no Chevrolet owner in the place to provide a more intense argument.

A farmer came in for a quick cup. The waitress asked, "What's the rush?"

"Planting beans this morning."

"You ought to wait for some rain," she advised.

"Nope. We got plenty of moisture at planting depth."

"Oh."

The farmer put his head down on the counter and moaned, "But it's way too early to plant beans."

◆   ◆   ◆

Maid-Rite talk usually was reasonably free of any threat to appetite. There were exceptions. A big, uncouth and foul-mouthed guy sometimes held down the end stool and when he was present the conversation turned to fishing, dogs and rivers. One morning, he and another unkempt man started talking about killing turtles and eating them.

"They've got seven kinds of meat from dark to real light."

A man at the other end of the counter piped up and said he had turtle gravy once. "It was the best I ever et."

Another wondered, unfortunately, how you get the meat out of a dead turtle. "Do you knock the shell to pieces with a hammer, or what?"

The big man, the turtle expert, said getting the meat out was easy. "You cut off the head and boil the shell. After that, well, there's this little trick I learnt as a kid. You put a garden hose under the shell after boiling, turn the water on full blast, and the shell separates from the meat just as neat as can be."

The conversation turned to another river reptile, the water moccasin. It petered out since poisonous snakes, as a breakfast topic, were even less appetizing than cutting off turtles' heads and boiling turtle meat.

◆   ◆   ◆

A minor emotional dust-up occurred when I removed the dented, crumpled green and white Washington plates IPT 559 from my VW and replaced them with crisp blue and white Iowa plates MCS 412 CEDAR.

Putting on Iowa places caused a distressing sensation, a sense of going backward. I kept the old Washington ones, pieces for my good medicine bag, remnants of another time.

◆   ◆   ◆

At times like these, my interior monologue turned to remembering my life farther west. The long highways, snowcaps and whitecaps. The Columbia River at Vantage, Washington, and the way it meandered south through the gap on the way to Hanford's old plutonium factories. Sage and the way it smelled when wet. Big snowy Mount Shasta at dawn coming into California from Oregon on I-5, looking forward to bacon and eggs at the Hi-Lo in Weed, and my skippy heart beat when I saw the San Francisco skyline filling the windshield. Oleanders in the median of Highway 99, the San Joaquin Valley expressway.

◆   ◆   ◆

At the tail end of my fading career in Seattle, I met a young reporter I called "the corporal" because that was his rank in the Marine Reserves. A funny guy, very energetic and idealistic, as the best young reporters tend to be, for a while. My corrosive cynicism amused him. He occasionally wrote me in Iowa with reports of his eroding enthusiasm. I wrote him in a pretty good mood.

"At ease. Smoke 'em if you got 'em! My big news on this Sunday morning in the middle of May is that during a bicycle ride west on the Cedar Bluff Road I saw the first corn of the season, out of the ground overnight about two inches. Not bad for a very dry spring. Times, for me, have changed. The lines are gone from my face. I'm fit. I sleep nine hours a night. I enjoy a beer. Everything but sex is in moderation here in southeastern Iowa. I am keeping a detailed journal. I talk to people as one human being to another rather than as a news reporter looking for good quotes.

"This morning at 7 o'clock I walked over to the Maid-Rite, my favorite hangout, for my habitual short stack and java. Twenty-five men were in the place. No women except for three waitresses. All but a few of the men wore work clothes, including one old man who looked like the Hollywood version of the grizzled farmer in overalls, except his were faded and worn from real work.

"The conversation, mostly banal, was of new corn and the efficiency of various weed-killing sprays. It sounded like a chemistry class. One old farmer, recently retired, harked to the days before herbicides and the epic fights with horseweeds using the old weapons of tractor-drawn tandem discs and cultivators. Everybody worried about lack of rain. One sissy in spiffy golf clothes looked in but left immediately.

"Don't be too despairing of newspaper work. Look at me. Fifty-two, semi-retired, happy as a dead hog in the sun. I spent only 30 years in journalism to get where I am."

◆   ◆   ◆

I took another bicycle ride west on the road to Cedar Bluff as far as the Mechanicsville Road. The countryside in the early evening was lovely. Farmers were in the field. Corn was up, barely out of the ground, the rows curving slightly. A sheen of green lay on the fields of new corn and the sun, a great orange orb, sank in the distance beyond the river. Except for the wind, all I could hear were the Raleigh's tires humming on the pavement and a very faint engine noise in the far distance. My mood was light and I thought of supper.

14

I spent a lot of time with my folks. I became part of their life of grocery shopping, errand running, visiting friends, doctor appointments and eating out. When I left Seattle, some people, the ones who had sentimental ideas about families, thought I was going back to Iowa to be with my folks for a while in their declining years. My dad was pushing 80. Mother was four years younger. I scoffed at suggestions of loving-son impulses, yet later I realized I had come home partly, at least, to spend time with them.

My dad Lysle, although physically robust, had a serious short-term memory problem which soon was diagnosed as the early stage of Alzheimer's disease. He slowly became disoriented although he frequently flashed his old charm and irascible sense of humor. Vivian, my mother, had been tormented much of her adult life by physical troubles, most related to heart damage from rheumatic fever when she was young. Mother was energetic mentally and frail physically.

As a boy, I spent more time with my dad ever since I was old enough to do a portion of a man's work. Picking corn, pulling weeds out of the beans, daily barnyard chores, riding shotgun on the corn planter and later working with him in his farm equipment repair and cemetery businesses. We had been close and easy going with each other, although not particularly forthcoming with affection and confidences. I distinctly remember his embarrassed admission that my mother was pregnant with Bill. I was 14.

He was a good man to work with, always fair, always pulling his weight without complaining. He was honest without being moralistic or self righteous. We never had a serious argument or disagreement.

One of my most intense memories of my dad was the overcast day in February, 1956, when I rode the Greyhound to Des Moines to join the army. I was in my second year at the university but was fatigued with school and decided to see the world. As the bus passed the Tiffin Cemetery west of Iowa City on U.S. 6, dad was standing by the highway and waved as the bus went by. He was at the cemetery on a grave digging job, and tears still come when I remember him there in gray coveralls on a cold and gloomy afternoon next to a snow-filled ditch.

I was reasonably close to my mother, but our family was emotionally reticent, a habit hard to break. However, as my dad sank deeper into Alzheimer's and found it hard to sustain a conversation, my mother and I grew closer. She became amazingly open in conversation. We spent a lot of time talking about my dad, the future, the past, my plans, relatives, my brothers. Mother's maiden name was Ratzlaff and her German upbringing expressed itself in a somewhat rigid attitude about right and wrong but she was not overbearing or unreasonable.

Mother and her parents talked very little about their past, not like my dad's side of the family. As a result, I knew almost nothing about their history. In addition, mother's family didn't have the equivalent of Uncle Lester, the Sanger family historian. About all I knew was that mother's dad, the taciturn Albert Ratzlaff, was of German stock, maybe originally from Bavaria. My mother's parents had farmed in southern Johnson County until 1924, when they moved to Iowa City.

Mother's mother, Ruth, maiden name Manasmith, was English. I was closest to her, by far, of any of my grandparents. She was warm and unconditional in her love for her grandchildren. Years later, seeking help from a psychoanalyst, I was told my troubles with "relationships" could be explained in one short sentence. I was looking for a replacement for Grandma Ruth.

◆   ◆   ◆

Mother and dad were married in 1933 at the Methodist parsonage on Jefferson Street in Iowa City. They were a handsome couple. Mother was dark and slim and pretty. She resembled Vivian Leigh.

Dad was ruddy, with a muscular build and light brown hair. Times were hard. The Depression and accompanying despair had taken hold, and after they were married my folks could not afford to live together. They stayed with their parents but since the families lived across from each other on West Benton Street the separation was not too onerous. They bought a moveable shack for $20, set it up near her parent's house and bunked in it for a while.

They soon began a tradition of moving. My mother left a handwritten account of where they had lived during more than 50 years of marriage. By 1940, when I was four, they had moved 15 times in seven years, often living in places with no electricity or running water when my dad worked for farmers as a hired man. By the time we moved to the farm in Cedar County in early 1945 my folks had moved a total of 22 times. Cedar County seemed to mark a change. They moved only nine more times, winding up in a house they bought not long before my dad retired in 1975 from the only decent job he ever had, as superintendent at Iowa City's municipal cemetery.

My dad always seemed to adore my mother but I recall numerous rough periods in their marriage, mostly arguments about money. These disputes were related to dad's reluctance to hold a steady job. He sometimes seemed to have a hard time growing up.

Dad, born in 1910, grew up in and around West Liberty, a small town 16 miles southeast of Iowa City in adjoining Muscatine County. His family moved to a farm near Iowa City in 1925. As a youth, he was a well known Iowa City High School football player, a lineman, small but aggressive. One of his several nicknames was "War Horse." He also had a certain fame as a chronic sleep-walker. In 1925, at age 16, he made the Iowa City paper when he sleep walked through a second-floor window and fell into a cellar window well, breaking his jaw. He told his parents he was dreaming about playing football. He was 73 before his next hospitalization.

His successful high school experience, both socially and on the football field, didn't translate into anything positive after graduation in the

Depression year of 1929. There was no work so he bounced between Iowa and California and points between as he and friends followed the wheat harvest in the Dakotas and Montana and the apple harvest in Washington state. Sometimes they simply went, like Jack Keroauc, not going to get somewhere, just going. Their favored ways of travel were freight trains and worn-out cars. Their favorite cars were a Model T and a beat-up Essex. Sometimes they walked or hitch-hiked.

Dad kept a journal on some of these adventures. A typical entry: "Too chilly to sleep. Asked to be put in jail to sleep but too many bugs. Hooked freight into Denver. Walked all night through Denver to keep warm. Oh, man was I tired."

After one extended stay in Southern California, which included working in a meat market at an A&P store in Santa Ana, dad became a food and vitamin faddist, an interest he maintained the rest of his life. During this Santa Ana period, he became a devotee of the Ehret diet, mostly fruits and vegetables, an absence of meat. Dad believed totally in Prof. Arnold Ehret's philosophy that "the clean foods of the Genesis" led to health and success in life. He bought these notions back with him to his parents' farm near Iowa City at the end of 1931. It was a bitter cold winter. Dad, his brothers and their friends were picking corn by hand for a little extra money. All had been converted (temporarily) to the Ehret "mucusless-diet healing system" which promised they would become perfect, 'physically, mentally and morally," if they stuck to it.

An evening meal Ehret-style after a grueling day of picking corn in the snow was not much to look forward to. The menu: five prunes, one tablespoon of peach juice and one cup of canned spinach. Before long the Ehret disciples drifted away from the sacred diet and began sneaking normal food to avoid semi-starvation and physical and mental collapse. Dad was profoundly disappointed but eventually drifted back himself to meat and potatoes.

◆   ◆   ◆

He tried to settle down after the marriage in '33. Even so, all his life he kept a belief that moving on changed things for the better. When life began to go bad or stale he would talk of heading out, always westward. It was corny but when dad heard a train whistle, his mood was immediately lighter and his eyes brightened, even into his late 70s.

He told stories of Santa Fe and Los Angeles in the '30s, Flagstaff, Arizona (which he called "Flag"), riding freights and sometimes the Super Chief passenger train (under the cars, on the brake rods, hence the phrase "riding the rods"), crossing the Mojave Desert, jail time in Needles, Calif., for stealing gas from a road grader. He figured that a black attendant on the Super Chief had saved his life by passing him a can of tomato juice while crossing the desert.

"No rattler I can't ride," he told his brother Lester, who was sometimes a traveling companion. Dad's last freight train ride was in 1933 when he went to the Black Hills looking for work. After two futile weeks of standing in soup lines and asking for handouts, he decided to come home. My mother wrote him a letter: "Darling, come home real soon. There is talk of work around here. I can't wait to see you. Be real careful coming home. Love, your little wife."

He told Lester of this last ride, and Lester included a description of it in a fond history he wrote in 1978 of my dad's life. In Lester's account, dad spotted an eastbound Red Ball freight picking up speed out of Rapid City as the sun was going down on a day in late August. He ran along the side tracks, lunged for the horizontal steel handle along the side of a car, scrambled up the ladder to the top. He "spider legged the catwalk on top of a galloping boxcar. A long tail of black smoke was whipping across the top of his car." The train snaked its way across the north rim of the Dakota Badlands through the dark of night, a lonesome whistle on the prairie.

◆   ◆   ◆

In 1943, dad acted on his daydreams and we moved to Toppenish, Washington, so he could work for his oldest brother, Kenneth, who was superintendent of the California Packing Corp. operation there. Dad was 4-F in the draft because of flat feet and a bum knee from a football injury. At that time married men with families were not at risk of being drafted. In February, four of us, five counting our Boston terrier Cubby, rode our '36 Hudson Terraplane west across the Rockies and the Blue mountains in winter. I remember snowstorms and roads blocked by slides and a semi-trailer hanging over a cliff west of La Grande, Oregon, on old U.S 30.

We lost Cubby early on, at a motel in Council Bluffs, Iowa. We left sadly without him. Without a word, at the Nebraska end of the Missouri River bridge, my dad turned around to go back to the motel for one last look. Dad bought Cubby in 1935 before I was born and we all considered him dad's dog. Back at the motel, Cubby was waiting.

(An aside about Cubby because he lived with us so long. In spite of a prickly personality, Cubby enjoyed a long and seemingly happy life. He was allowed to roam free and in the process sired dozens of offspring, quite a few litters in cooperation with my English shepherd Lassie. Cubby, returning from a ramble one afternoon during the summer of 1948, was killed while crossing busy U.S. 6 in front of our farm on the edge of Tiffin, Iowa, a small town west of Iowa City. A witness, a friend of our family, told us a driver in a Buick swerved, not to miss Cubby but to hit him.)

But, back to the 1943 way west to Washington. My folks bought me an Indian head dress in Rawlins, Wyoming. My dad was cited for speeding in La Grande, a town my mother always said was her all-time favorite place without ever explaining why.

It was a farm job in Washington's Yakima Valley. Both my folks loved living there in the wide open spaces with a view of Mount Adams from our front yard. They made friends easily and within the limits of wartime gasoline rationing we spent time in the Cascades on overnight trips. In spite of their happiness in Washington and the excitement of a new place, after one year we moved back to Iowa so my dad could work for his dad on a farm near Wapello south of Iowa City. Homesickness was the official reason. I think I knew moving back was a mistake and that homesickness also was a mistake. My mother always said moving back definitely was a mistake, one of the most serious of their married life.

The "mistake" had something to do with going back to work for a domineering father after finding a good life and good friends in a new place.

◆   ◆   ◆

Dad lasted one year working for his dad. Adult sons and fathers usually are not a happy blend. My grandparents sold the Wapello farm and moved to Iowa City. We moved to the 160-acre tenant farm south of Tipton. It was "on the shares, 50-50," which meant my dad did the work and the landlord got half of the proceeds. My mother called the landlord, whose first name I have forgotten, "Peaches" Taylor. That was because there was one peach tree. My mother picked the peaches and the landlord showed up and asked for half.

◆   ◆   ◆

My dad never got over his restlessness. When he was almost 60, I rushed to Iowa City from Honolulu when mother was perilously ill with a pulmonary embolism. He and I sat on spring afternoon on the grass outside the university's general hospital and talked about what we would do if mother died. Dad said he would bury mother in a country cemetery near where she was born in southern Johnson County, quit his job and head west.

He recited poetry. Shakespeare, some Longfellow, Tennyson's "Crossing the Bar," and the poem about "Old Ironsides...Give her to the god of storms, the lightning and the gale." His favorite, judging from frequency of quotation, was James Oliver Hungerford's "Pot Luck Partners," which I heard so often growing up I can recite most of it from memory.

"We've traveled heaps of tangled trails ol' pard and seen some life. We've followed old adventure's lure, and drained the cup of thrills. We've tramped the trails from icy Nome to spicy Mexico. We've busted bronc and ridden herd and seen the steers stampede, and watched men die without a word, the trigger finger breed."

Often he recited only the last lines:

"We've had our fling at life, ol' pard, our strenuous days are done;

"We've staked our all on fortune's card, and sometimes lost and won;

"We've played the game o' give and take, and took whatever came;

"Good luck or bad, or make or break, we've always played the game."

He had a tender aspect too. Another of his favorite poems, and I don't know who wrote it, was about a woman's love. "A lone man's companion, a sad man's cordial, a chilly man's fire, nothing like it under the canopy of heaven."

◆   ◆   ◆

His favorite reward for a hard day's work was to take my brother and me to a western movie. I learned a code of conduct watching Randolph Scott and Wild Bill Elliott and later on James Stewart, Glenn Ford, Gary Cooper, Richard Widmark, Gregory Peck. I learned it was all right, even noble, to be alone and to be footloose. I liked Jimmy Ringo's (Gregory Peck) comment in "The Gunfighter": "I'm 33 years old and I don't even own a decent watch."

As an adult, those western movie images directed my day dreams. Swinging into the saddle, pebbles clattering as a horse lunged up an incline, the sound a Winchester lever action rifle makes as a round is jacked into the chamber. But it was a long time until I saw my ideal western movie scene, one I had imagined inside my head but never had seen on a screen until I watched "Lonely Are the Brave," a Kirk Douglas western made in 1962. On the run, Douglas saddles his horse, a Winchester in the saddle scabbard. He talks sweetly and briefly to the woman. He admits his loner philosophy. He never wanted a house or pots and pans. All he ever wanted was her. He realizes he would not have been good for her. He kisses her and swings into the saddle. The lights of a small town are low in the background, a mountain range behind. The cowboy looks at the woman from the saddle, spurs his horse toward the mountains. The scene lasts three minutes.

◆   ◆   ◆

Dad liked women. At parties, he was with the women, not much with the men. He was muscular and good looking with a high-spirited sense of humor. He was a good listener. My guess was he had had many girl friends, starting in high school and continuing during his vagabond years until his marriage. He spoke occasionally of dark-eyed senoritas met on the road in New Mexico and California. My sense was that his happiest years were spent in high school and during his foot-loose years before he became a husband and father.

My dad was a dreamy man, never careful about his financial or occupational future. My 2nd ex-wife's outbursts when she accused me of trying to finish my dad's life for him probably contained a large measure of truth. He got married and settled down. His restlessness found expression in dreaming out loud and taking his sons to western movies. I kept the romance alive by leaving jobs and women to pursue notions as vague and dreamy as my dad's.

◆   ◆   ◆

My mother was not a dreamer. She emphasized real goals, achievable ones, a more realistic way to happiness. Steady work, payment of debts, decent furniture. She had a strong sense of order. She didn't brag much, except to agree she was a very good cook, along Germanic lines of potatoes in various forms, candied yams, roast beef, pork roast, noodles, chicken gravy, roast chicken, peerless pies and cakes.

Clean and neat to a fault, she didn't sleep well if she knew some part of her house was less than perfect. Lint under the refrigerator or a disorderly back shelf in the linen closet made her uneasy. She pushed herself hard on cleaning and redecorating projects as if her life depended on it. A couple of times I was afraid she would suffer a fatal attack trying to wash the inside of a storm window or the wall behind the refrigerator. She flew the flag on December 7 and Armistice Day and she always made sure birds who visited her yard in the winter had food and water.

When we moved to a new place, my folks always cleaned it up. Barnyard, house yard, inside and out. Sometimes we only stayed a year but when we left it was tidy, much tidier than when we came.

Mother was puritanical. Sex talk upset her. To her, women were not pregnant. They were "p.g." Growing up, I thought my mother was possessive and too much concerned with money and security. More recently, I have realized she was trying to cope with a dreamy man who thought too much of the days of dark-eyed senoritas and too much about moving on. Not enough about sticking to a job and making a living. They were frequently broke. Mother worried. Dad seemed to assume something would come along.

The something good dad was waiting for was a long time coming. In 1952, when I was a sophomore in high school, we were living in a rundown old farmhouse east of Iowa City that had no indoor toilet and no running hot water.

My folks had no economic security in their married life until dad was 53 in 1963 and landed the job as Iowa City's chief gravedigger. After that, although I was long gone from home, it was clear life had become brighter for mother. Life was even easier after retirement. Dad had a decent Social Security check, a cushy health insurance plan because of his city employment and a small pension. Their house was paid for. They were frugal and had no debts. Until dad began to lose his bearings, they were on Easy Street.

◆   ◆   ◆

My parents were likeable, friendly people with simple tastes. They paid their bills on time when they had the money. They were punctual. Storm windows went up early and the car got winterized in the fall. They didn't smoke or drink, although my mother liked a cold beer on a summer day or a glass of sweet wine with dinner. Neither was worldly, or materialistic beyond what was needed for reasonable comfort.

Neither one was a know-it-all. They didn't give advice very often. Mother was disapproving about strong drink and hanging out with suspicious women. The only advice I recall from dad was one very cold winter day as we were getting ready for a grave digging job. Dad suggested I wear a cotton T-shirt. "Otherwise, it won't make any difference how many layers you have on. You won't be warm without a T-shirt."

He maintained something like a sense of humor, even as he sank into the abyss of Alzheimer's. Old friends would visit and often he didn't recognize them. When they got up to leave, he seemed to dimly realize he should say something friendly. His usual parting line was: "Drop in whenever you're in town."

My dad finished high school but except for a very brief stint at a small college in Minnesota on a football scholarship he didn't go to school again. His three brothers, all professional engineers, left Iowa

City after college. Lester was in Lincoln; Merle lived in Southern California; Kenneth moved around on the West Coast. Dad's sisters, except for Wanda, left Iowa City. Moneta lived in the Quad-Cities and Ardis in the New York area. Alta, the oldest of the girls, died young, at age 24 in 1933. My feeling was that dad, until he landed the real job at the city cemetery, felt left far behind by his brothers. He sometimes had a forlorn look in photos taken at family reunions.

My mother left school at about age 14 because of rheumatic fever. Mother never worked outside the home, except for odds and ends like a few days packing peas and sweet corn at the Del Monte plant when they lived in the Yakima Valley.

Her only sibling, Daryl, the World War II medic, lived in nearby Cedar Rapids. A gentle, friendly man, he was a tool and die-maker at a small manufacturing firm.

My parents were not religious in the devout sense. They were proud that they were charter members of a big and rich, socially-prominent Presbyterian congregation. But not for reasons of Christian faith. Mostly, they liked being part of a congregation that included doctors who were high up in the university's medical school. My dad always said some people had clubs for their social life but he and mother had the church.

Neither particularly encouraged or discouraged Duane and me about going to college. They were generous with living space and meals after we became college students. They respected education; they were not dazzled by it. They did not pressure us to go into any particular line of work. We were on our own. I think both were amazed when I became a newspaper reporter and stuck to it. That line of work was completely beyond their understanding.

They came to adulthood during the Depression and always worried about money. They watched society change from a family orientation to one where divorce became increasingly frequent. My brothers and I all were divorced. They had the heartache of Bill going to prison and the death of my son, Sam, their first grandchild, in 1982 at age 17.

Sam suffered severe brain damage at birth and spent almost his entire life in a California state institution. My folks regretted that all their sons lived far away. They never had the chance to watch any of their grandchildren grow up.

They soldiered on. When I came home, all of a sudden I remembered something I had read. When you are young you observe others, and when you are older there comes a point when people start observing you. When I came home the last time it was different. I wasn't the child anymore. They watched me, waited for me to make decisions, leaned on me.

◆   ◆   ◆

We had fun. In their big red four-door Buick Century, my dad's pride and joy, we roamed within 25 to 30 miles of Iowa City. A favorite area was southeast of Iowa City around Kalona where my mother grew up among farmers of German ancestry. The Amish live there now. During these jaunts we often stopped for lunch. A favorite stop was the Colony Inn in the Amana Colonies west of Iowa City where we dined family style on old-fashioned German food. Other favorites included cafeterias and buffets and little diners scattered through the area.

My folks seldom went to movies. They didn't attend sporting events. Eating out was their recreation. They liked variety and they enjoyed watching people.

We visited relatives and friends during quick stops, usually accompanied by coffee and pie. I think, though, the most fun was on Mother's Day Sunday '88. We started the outing by looking for a place to have lunch. I suggested the Maid-Rite in Tipton and looked forward to a good, cheap meal in familiar surroundings. We got there after 1 p.m. The Maid-Rite was closed. We tried the Cove down on 80 by the old farm; it was wall to wall people. We finally stopped at a truck stop farther east on 80. We had an indifferent meal. I paid, as part of my new role of person taking charge. It was a warm sunny day in mid-May. After we ate, a man in the parking lot told us he had driven through a hell of a storm farther west. We looked and saw a low blackness on the horizon. We didn't pay it much attention.

For some time, I had wanted to visit the tiny country cemetery where my dad's maternal grandparents were buried. It was nearby, and we drove over. I always drove by then because dad had reached the point where he thought everybody but him should stop at intersections. "I'm tired of stopping. Let somebody else stop for a while," he said. After Mother heard that comment a couple of times she took away the car keys and he never drove again.

We found the cemetery, called North Liberty, and leaving mother in the Buick my dad and I walked over to a cluster of gravestones. They were old and the names and dates were worn and hard to read. Finally, I found what I assumed was the stone marking the grave of dad's grandfather. George Bates, died July 7, 1888, probably the father of my dad's mother Nellie.

Suddenly, as we looked at the tombstone, the air became heavy and very still. I looked behind us. The faintly ominous cloud bank far to the west we had seen from the truck stop had grown to a towering and boiling expanse of black-green meanness that was moving very fast toward us. I could see columns of dust hundreds of feet high in the fields under the cloud and thought maybe after all these years of looking at frightening storms I would finally see a funnel cloud. Mother was gesturing wildly from the front seat of the Buick. Dad and I ran toward the car. Dad was having fun. He ran gleefully through the knee-high grass, grinning ear to ear.

We jumped into the car and tore out of the cemetery hitting the gravel road hard and turning east away from the storm. I had read that you could usually outrun a tornado, which moved about 40 miles an hour across the ground even though air might be whirling at 500 miles an hour inside the funnel. Well, I could tell this storm was moving toward us a lot faster than 40 miles an hour. We were moving a lot faster than that and making no headway against the approaching cloud. We came up against what looked like a dead end. I looked for a place to turn around, wondering if a two-ton Roadbuster '75 Buick could take a tornado head on. Then, I saw it was not a dead end after all. The road turned south which put us at right angles to the storm. I took a good look. More dust than I had ever seen was moving across the fields. Wind, hail and rain slammed into us. Visibility fell to 15 or 20 feet.

I saw a shallow driveway with an overhanging dirt bank. I nudged the Buick as close as possible to the bank hoping it would afford some protection. The big car rocked sideways and seemed to be lifting off its springs. The screaming wind and clattering hail made it impossible to talk. My mother sat next to me, scared stiff. I wondered if we should abandon the car and lie in the ditch as tornado experts advised. I looked in the back seat. Dad had leaned forward and put his hand on mother's shoulder. Fairly quickly, in a minute or two, the fury passed. We drove back to Iowa City, marveling at uprooted trees, downed power lines and wrecked farm buildings. We were thrilled to the teeth. Two twisters had blown through that part of Johnson and Cedar counties. Eight hogs were killed when a barn collapsed.

"One Mother's Day I won't forget," my mother said. What I liked best was my dad's grin as he ran through the high grass and the way he stayed calm and put his hand on my mother's shoulder.

15

With June came summer. And with summer something else, the beginning in earnest of the '88 drought, the worst dry spell in Iowa since the Dust Bowl days of the 1930s. Since I wasn't a farmer and didn't depend on farmers, the effect on me, aside from sympathy, was mostly aesthetic. As the drought worsened, the fields of plenty withered to something not so pretty. The early summer weather was almost Mediterranean.

One personal drawback of the hot weather was that noises from people living around me became annoying with windows open and tempers inflamed by the non-stop heat. On balance I liked it in the trailer court. People left me alone. The heat did make me peevish occasionally, along with a rising level of testosterone which made me testy. One afternoon, I tried to find something listenable on my car's AM radio. WMT Cedar Rapids was playing request rock 'n' roll but the station's idea of rock 'n' roll was music from Gidget beach blanket movies, or the standbys "Moon Glow" and "Moon River." Another popular choice was the mawkish "Donna, Donna, I had a girl, Donna was her name." The sponsor of the show was a religious bookstore in Cedar Rapids.

I knew I was in the land of the bland, stuck in the late '50s or early '60s. Girls when driving with their boyfriends, sat close. A smugness and sameness everywhere I looked. Picasso's comment about the Spanish seemed apt. A people of "legendary immobility."

I decided to follow Norman Vincent Peale's advice. When bored or listless or depressed, think positively and do something positive. Take a shower, reflect on the Good Book, mow the yard, give the dog a bath. I took all the wheels off my car, and sanded them and painted them on both sides, inside and out, including the spare. I used two coats of expensive anti-rush chrome paint. After that I put two coats of flat black, my favorite color, on bumpers front and rear. My Rabbit looked spiffy. I got more pleasure from this busy work than anything else I had done in a long time, except for eating cole slaw mixed with walnuts at Victorian House.

◆   ◆   ◆

My uncle Lester passed through from Lincoln. He told a story I liked, partly because of my critical mood. Lester was in Dayton, Ohio, visiting a daughter. He went to get a haircut. The barber asked where he was from. "Lincoln, Nebraska," Les replied.

"Do you have to live there?" the barber asked. Les was annoyed. He was a Lincoln booster.   *Explain*   *Why the anamosity*

◆   ◆   ◆

Following the Rev. Dr. Peale's advice, I wrote two upbeat letters. Never believe everything you read in letters from friends far away. You don't have a clue. The correspondent likely will be gilding the lily. One of the letters went to Tom, my city editor in Seattle. He was nick-named "The Slumbering Giant" by people who liked him. Those who didn't called him "The Man in the Empty Suit." Tom had left Seattle to work at the *Los Angeles Times*. He and I had been drinking buddies who didn't always see eye to eye in the city room. My feeling that journalism was a cacophony of the irrelevant, trivial, silly and repetitious didn't sit well with a city editor.

I had been the Slumberer's best man at his second wedding. We remained friends in spite of occasional office disagreements. I assumed this affinity was based on our Midwestern upbringings. Tom was a small town Hoosier. Talking to him on a bar stool was like conversations in the dark City High bus on the way home from track meets, or intimate chats with male friends in cars on late summer nights. Not especially cerebral or contemplative but pleasant and without conflict. Relaxed, amusing, lots of gossip. Basically comforting, with no danger of serious dispute as long as the subjects stayed clear of occupational topics. He could take a joke.

One night we sat at the Silver Stein under the monorail near the old *Post-Intelligencer* building. We were watching a Sonics basketball game on TV. The announcer said something about the Sonics not scoring for more than two minutes. I turned to an assistant city editor there with us and said, "That's nothing. Tom hasn't scored for two years."

No need to be on your guard with a buddy from Indiana.

"Life here is not bad," I wrote Tom. "I'm restless, though, and at times can see myself jumping out of bed some morning and prepping my VW for a long trip west on 80. I think whatever I do I will keep this place as a base because it is cheap and I kind of like living here. I think I'm living on $700 a month. I like seeing my folks. I like Cedar County. The countryside has great presence and dignity. It is familiar to me.

"I came here to work in a book about life in a little farming town. I started pretty strong but the project has taken a few convoluted turns, from oral history to personal odyssey. I sense there is a story here. It has not dawned on me what it is. I have a chance to write something. It is up to me."

◆   ◆   ◆

Another letter went to John and Karen who had left Seattle to work for a Catholic mission organization in Lima, Peru. They quit good jobs, sold everything, packed up three young children and flew to Lima. Their motivation, they admitted with some embarrassment, was "at least, somewhat, altruistic."

"A warmish day. I am at my concrete block converted trailer park launderette efficiency apartment listening to periodic arguments from the poor whites in the next trailer arguing about who stole the cigarettes, or whose turn was it to change the baby's diaper. My life has become, in Madame R's description, an Iowa version of a John Updike novel. I am not sure what she means by that, but Mrs. R is unfailingly literary.

"A few setbacks. A promising romance fizzled. The woman was married although not living with her husband. This information should be filed under 'the rubbish of personal lives.' I feel at home here and miss very little about Seattle. Is that odd? I lived there 15 years, had a good job and many close friends.

"One of my projects here is to read my journals which I have kept since 1953. I have all of them here in my bunker and I must say that reading them makes me realize how much better off I am now than I have been at most times in my life. I feel loose and free."

◆   ◆   ◆

As summer came on hot and dry and the drought tightened, I listened to classical music from Iowa City, stopped at the air-conditioned library on broiling afternoons to read the *New Yorker* and *Scientific American*. I checked out books on Irish terrorism (a subject that had interested me ever since a brief visit to Belfast) and AIDS. None of these subjects interfered with my quiet and incredibly boring and satisfying life in Tipton, Cedar County, Iowa.

◆   ◆   ◆

When in a reflective mood, I scanned my one-room digs, like a movie camera panning a scene. In one corner, next to the wall gas furnace, was a mannequin's leg, booty from a day scrounging with Christine. A wall map of the U.S. Interstate Highway System next to the furnace. Nearby, a U-shaped bicycle carrier that fit on the back of my car, a cardboard box full of audio tapes, the portable Sony radio/tape player. A foot stool which had been a little wooden crate for Schweppes tonic. I found it on the beach at Lanikai when I lived on Oahu. My Weihrauch German air rifle hung over the door (handy for silently dinging barking dogs), and a single-shot Harrington & Richardson rifle was slung under a bulletin board by the door, along with my shooting vest, leather ammo bag and canteen. My old Winchester 25.35 lever action, the most valuable thing I owned after my car, was in storage at my brother's place in Fresno. The Raleigh Super Course bicycle, with its fine Reynolds 531 frame, from Nottingham, England, leaned against a closet door. Minimal clothes, mostly khaki wash pants and blue work shirts, a few flannel and chamois shirts from L.L. Bean and Eddie Bauer, a worn out brown tweed jacket and two aloha shirts. A Metropolitan Museum of Art calendar and a U.S. Geological Survey map of Cedar County were taped on the closet door.

A few reference files sat on a folding aluminum table borrowed from Christine, along with a pocket-sized Pentax 35mm camera and Panasonic mini-cassette tape recorder. I had a few books on the kitchen counter which extended into the sitting room. Mostly the books were Manhattan Project and other atomic bomb histories, a leather Bible my folks gave me in 1943. Two lamps that folded for travel.

With the books were framed photos of my daughter, my brothers and my folks. My parents were many years younger in the photograph. Next to them was a gold framed photo of Gary Cooper in his role as Will Kane in *High Noon*, wearing a six-gun and a tin star. A shiny black ashtray from Pompeii's Grotto on Fisherman's Wharf in San Francisco held change and some pieces of sagebrush from eastern Washington. I ground the sage between my fingers when I got lonely for open spaces.

Stuck to a fiberboard wall above my work area were art photos, manuscript notes, a tiny watercolor of the Seine. The watercolor of a bridge and the Paris skyline was a gift from my daughter after her first summer in Paris. I owned a really nice George Shane oil, eight inches by ten, on Masonite, of an Iowa farm in winter. The late George Shane, a regionally well-known painter and a writer at the *Des Moines*

Register, was my brother Duane's father-in-law once upon a time. Above everything was a moody photo of a Montana highway and mountains in a storm, shot through the windshield of my gone and lamented '65 VW.

Against this wall, the bathroom wall, on tables borrowed from my folks, were my Juki printer and Kaypro computer, a traveler's alarm clock, an old red Western Electric Bell System rotary dial telephone. Behind me as I sat at the computer was the sway-backed double bed and to my right a bullet-riddled man-sized target, and next to it a National Geographic map of The Four Corners of Utah, Colorado, Arizona and New Mexico.

In the kitchen, a just-about shot Teflon skillet, a small white sauce pan, an Italian white china plate with a classy narrow blue stripe circling the edge, a Swedish wooden dish drainer, tea kettle, fairly fancy stainless steel Thermos and coffee maker, a Lola dish scrubber brush and odds and ends of silverware and other dishes, enough for three people max.

In the bathroom, next to the shower, I had one good bath towel.

By the front door along the wall were a red gasoline can, two quarts of Pennzoil 10-40 motor oil, a bicycle tire pump. Leaning against the wall was my ancient American Tourister brown imitation leather suitcase, and hanging from wall pegs were a cheap bag from Seoul and a blue Finnair shoulder bag bought on the run as Dr. Dick, blonde Janice and I rushed for an airplane in Helsinki that was loading for New York.

This inventory, not including the furniture, I could get into or attach to my VW.

Otherwise, the room held a ratty sofa, a ratty rocking chair I draped clothes on and two cardboard packing boxes for the printer and computer. I used the packing boxes as end tables. The outer walls were paneled in imitation dark wood. The wall between the main room and bathroom was paneled in imitation cork. One big window looked out on Lynn Street and the houses across. A small window by the kitchen stove showed a trailer and the corner of a field. There were three horizontal glass slits close to the ceiling above the bed and another in the bathroom. These reminded me of rifle slits in a frontier fort. The floor was covered with what looked like outdoor carpet, a brown floral pattern. The shower was not bad and the indoor plumbing worked okay. I had no television set and hadn't since my second divorce.

My bunker diet resembled Ehret, I guess, and ran to green peppers, cucumbers, apples, bananas, prunes, raisins, all fresh or semi-fresh, organic when I could afford it. In cans were stewed tomatoes, black beans, lentil and vegetable soup and tuna fish. I was fond of brown rice and black beans, whole grain wheat bread and rice or oat breakfast food with a handful of Spanish peanuts or broken raw cashews. Farmers or Colby longhorn cheese. I steered clear of butter (solid cow oil) and spread instead with soybean margarine. I drank less beer than I had in years. When I did I stuck to Old Style or Blue, maybe a bottle of Special Export for special occasions. Mostly, I drank tea at home, black coffee at the Maid-Rite. Ty-Phoo tea when I could get it, brand loyalty left over from living in St. Ives, Cornwall.

I was spending around $700 a month, and living well. Breakfast out every morning, an occasional movie. I made very few long distance phone calls, but wrote many letters. The biggest ticket items, aside from my daughter's college costs and travel expenses, were rent, car insurance and medical insurance. I had no income except for several thousand dollars a year in interest and stock dividends. My current life style would end when my savings evaporated but for the time being I was living as I pleased. Over the years, people had made fun of my stingy personality, emotional as well as financial. My stock response was that I didn't buy things; I bought time. It was costing me $38,000 in lost wages to live in Tipton for a year. I didn't buy stereos or gadgets or costly restaurant meals. I kept good tires on my car and I kept the engine tuned so it would start at minus 20. I maintained zero balance when possible on my credit card and always had a valid passport. I didn't like to spend more than $5 on a meal out unless dessert was something special. What I had accomplished by this frugality had brought me more pleasure than all the gee-gaws of materialism I saw in other lives. Traveling lighter, faster and farther.

I didn't go to taverns much anymore. I didn't want to go alone and there was no one to call. Conn had flown, and Christine was married with a mansion to run. For recreation I wrote old girl friends. I could be intimate and no strings attached. No cost. We had been over the dangerous ground already.

"I was drinking beer last night, lounging in my plastic chair in front of my concrete block hut, catching what breeze there was on a hot sultry night. I thought about phoning you. It was late and I went to bed instead. I had been listening to a country music station, and country music reminds me of us at Gilley's Place in Pasadena, Texas. What a night. Lone Star and the cowboy 2-step. And, yeah, I think you got it right when you wrote that probably you didn't love your ex-husband anymore after you became indifferent to his new wife. Funny how long it takes. And, yeah, you likely would hang onto your men friends longer if you would put out more, but I can understand why you don't. You are old fashioned and think that hitting the sheets really means something. I guess it does, maybe, you might say, sometimes. Sex raises the stakes." ✱ M vs F

◆　　　◆　　　◆

The bicycle rides kept me together, put form on my days. It must be true about exercise manufacturing a good-mood chemical. Riding in the country I decided that farmers in Cedar County had it best, at least the ones who weren't going under. Farming was the basic industry. The county depended on them. They were an nobility in overalls. There was grudging admission among the town vassals that farmers were important. The country people had the rhythm of the seasons. They had the serenity of the countryside. If of a solitary nature, what more could one ask for than a nice-running big tractor, a day in the field with a break for lunch?

◆   ◆   ◆

Christine, in one of her more negative moments, had called rural Iowa a sliced white bread and mayonnaise society. One day, down for the eight count, I confessed to my Kaypro:

State of mind. Outside it's 86 going on 96. Inside, probably 106. I am sitting in my Hanes boxer shorts drinking beer in front of the wide open door. The white trash in the trailer next door are fighting about money and WHY DON'T THAT BABY SHUT UP! I cycled down to the p.o. to mail a handful of letters. Since the first of the month I have written 44 letters and cards, hoping the world will hear me and write back. I feel drained, dry, dusty, sick and tired, horny, lonely, not old, but getting old, and running out of room to turn in. I can still hit a beer can stuck in a tree from 70 feet with the H&R single shot firing .38 reloads. So can any girl with 10 minutes instruction. Romance dimmed and became what Tom calls "a second fiddle situation." I guess I am looking for a woman of my own. I have decided my churlish attitude about Tipton is dumb and banal and not saleable since I am not a celebrity and nobody wants to pay me for writing about anything but traffic fatals and bank stickups. My idea of writing a novel about a hack reporter has lost momentum. I can't seem to get past the first paragraph. I recall Dr. Dick's comment that anyone who doesn't write for money is jerking off and except for wondering how Emily Dickinson fits that scenario I agree with Dick all the way. Maybe it is age but I sense my maneuvering is room is getting smaller. It could be an illusion, probably is, but the physical bigness of the West is comforting. Plenty of room to fumble at the goal line, recover and go on to score.

◆   ◆   ◆

It was at this point that I called Judith Wacha up the street, the newcomer, to set up an interview. After talking to her on her front porch early on a very warm June day, I returned to the bunker faintly encouraged. While thinking about lunch I heard a familiar whisper. It was the highway calling. My mood chemistry flipped. Life was not so bad. On my own, not beholden to anyone, the money I saved living in a converted launderette I could spend on Greyhound tickets to either coast. The world was my oyster. I was inspired by my dad's "Spirit of '29" when he hit the rails west. Contrast was life. I was free to go. Thank God and Greyhound, I'm gone! As Charles Bukowski said, "Packing was always a good time."

16

B y the time I returned to my bunker in mid-August, six weeks gone, I felt like a man living in self-imposed exile. Tipton became a place to sleep and to complain about. The West Coast had the effect of disconnecting me from Cedar County. My attitude was distant, vacant, like a visitor. I waited for time to bring a sign. A sign might be a telephone call from Dr. Dick asking me to meet him in Lisbon or Berlin, or a wild hair in the night to leave for somewhere else, maybe Montana or upstate New York. Even though being West again had made me dissatisfied, the experience had not provided escape. I had not found an opening. I felt like a crewman aboard "The Flying Dutchman," doomed to an eternity of seeking a harbor.

◆　　　◆　　　◆

Scribbles in a travel notebook. As the Greyhound left the Iowa City station in early July and headed north up Dubuque Street for the inter-state, I passed George's Buffet and Hamburg Inn No. 2, places where I had been ordering hamburgers, black coffee and Old Style on draft for 30 years off and on, give or take. I looked to the right when we got to I-80, east toward Cedar County before the bus turned left and west. I felt sad, but excited too, and thought perhaps Iowa City and environs were home after all. I was getting homesick before the bus left the city limits.

In August, 1958, I had departed Iowa City in a happy and expectant mood aboard a Greyhound headed for San Francisco. On that August day I couldn't wait to be gone. History repeated. Iowa City was quickly forgotten. By the time we crossed the Missouri at Omaha, the traveling life held me tight. West of Grand Junction, Colo., well into the stark

Colorado Plateau, I was thinking the West looked pretty good. As we paralleled the Colorado River I wondered if in all this space there was a place for me. By Las Vegas, I was getting pumped for California. At the breakfast stop in Barstow I called ahead to my Los Angeles connection, former reporter colleague and friend Carol. I told her the bus was on time and we could meet outside the station at the corner of 6th and Los Angeles.

Carol had been the longtime lover of a newspaper friend of mine in Seattle. She was an earnest and guileless woman who wore flannel shirts, blue jeans and sensible shoes when she and I had been reporters together. She was bespectacled, hard working, good humored, good looking, not provocative sexually (in spite of red hair), perhaps a touch naïve. A few weeks before I left Tipton, she telephoned me out of the blue and wondered what I was up to. I told her I was planning a trip to the West Coast. She suggested I stay at her place in north Los Angeles for a night or two on my way to Seattle. She told me she was a different person than the one I remembered. She and my friend had split, and she had blossomed into a regular shopper at Neiman Marcus, was a frequenter of Beverly Hills and was "hard-bodied from working out."

One night in her backyard pool, a few days after my arrival, and following a few gins-and-tonic, she said she was taking time off from the *Los Angeles Times* to make a sentimental trip to her Nevada hometown. She asked if I wanted to go along after my Seattle visit. I said sure and the next day I left for Seattle.

◆   ◆   ◆

In central Washington, as I drove away from the Yakima River and the brown hills, I thought of the good times there and sadly realized it might be a while before I was back again. I noticed that my friends in Seattle talked about golf and baseball, opera and children and had gone on with their lives in my absence. Sometimes I missed my Tipton routine, my path between the bunker, Maid-Rite, library and Victorian

House. In Seattle, I read a biography of Grant Wood by James M. Dennis. The book about Grant Wood put Iowa, especially the Iowa City area where he painted and died, into an intellectual framework for me. It made an Iowa regionalist of me, made Iowa seem more like home, the right place. I decided Iowa was where I lived now.

"For the most part only the light characters travel. Who are you that have no task to keep you at home?" Ralph Waldo Emerson wrote that. When I first read it, I agreed with him, thus rejecting my entire philosophy of traveling light and frequently. I dropped Emerson as the southbound Greyhound from Seattle to Los Angeles crossed the California line on I-5. I liked the sensation of movement, of being in California again. I could see Mount Shasta in the early morning light and I looked forward to the lovely brown, green, snow-capped country between the Oregon line and the Sacramento River.

As the trip went on, to Los Angeles, to Nevada with Carol, and back to Los Angeles, I was looking always for a place for me. Best of all was the time in Nevada, where we went because Carol was looking for her youth and maybe a book in the closed-down Kennecott copper pits and smelter around Ely, Ruth and McGill. Nevada's promotional slogan was "where the Old West still lives." The slogan rang true.

We stayed up late in Nevada's 24-hour society, drank Coor's and danced to live bands. We walked in the sagebrush desert and shot my big Ruger Blackhawk revolver at tin cans. We visited ghost towns and cemeteries, made late night and early morning love in the Jailhouse Motel. On the way to Ely from Las Vegas on U.S. 93, her Chrysler almost out of gas, we found a crossroads oasis called Major's Place, where U.S. 93, 50 and 6 intersect at a place of almost unimaginable distance and view. We kept going back to Major's to drink Coor's, listen to the country western jukebox and talk to cowboys and sheepherders and prospectors who came to Major's at night. Sometimes Carol jabbered in Spanish learned at Ely High.

The stars one night were so bright we could have read a newspaper in their light. Carol walked across U.S. 50 and impulsively lay down on the pebbly shoulder next to the westbound lane. I lay with her and she showed me the constellations, from a horizontal perspective, our own planetarium. I suggested we give up Los Angeles and Tipton, the two of us, and buy Major's Place where we would get a free year-around gander at Wheeler Peak. She was not enthusiastic. I guess she was afraid she would miss the Santa Monica Freeway and the morning view of downtown Los Angeles coming down the Glendale Freeway. "Kind of a fairyland view sometimes," she said. Carol could quote Lord Tennyson's "Idylls of the King," so I figured she wasn't completely beyond the realm of the sensitive.

◆   ◆   ◆

I was nervous about returning to the corn and bean fields after Nevada's limitless horizon. Even Los Angeles, a place I found sometimes fascinating but not at all endearing, held my interest longer than usual. I drove to the observatory at Griffith Park because I wanted a look at the city and a place to think for a while. This digression was a way to avoid the bus station for a while. The observatory gave up no secrets, and by the following day the hundreds of miles that had flowed past the bus window had dulled me to anything but a desire to stretch out for a long nap.

◆   ◆   ◆

In Iowa, it was almost too hot and humid to think. Even so, I dimly understood the Victorian summer had ended for me on the Fourth of July when the Gelms and I sat on their back porch drinking beer and watching fireworks. By summer, I mean laughter, good times and good feelings. I came back to learn the Gelms were moving to their other bed and breakfast in Bellevue, 65 miles northeast on the Mississippi, not far from Dubuque.

Their explanation was that Bellevue was a better spot for tourism because of the river and the hilly, scenic country around Dubuque, a city with a history going back to the late 1700s, something unusual in Iowa. Bellevue was a pretty little town, but lacked the gritty rural reality of Tipton. Christine told me she had done in Tipton what she had set out to do, which was to bring the Victorian House back from the near-dead and to start a viable business. My participation in their life ended, along with the benefits of knowing them. I was a lonely guy in Snotpit.

I felt disjointed because of the traveling and, worst of all, I returned with no dream of the West. None, at least, I could translate into action at the end of my Cedar County sojourn.

Carol formally nixed my half-serious suggestion we buy Major's and look at Wheeler Peak and endless vistas of sagebrush for the rest of our lives. Beyond missing the Santa Monica Freeway, she was unwilling to give up the *Los Angeles Times'* velvet coffin of good pay, high prestige, generous pension, half-price photo processing and awfully good cafeteria food. Plus, she liked Los Angeles, and I figured, yeah, difference of opinion is what makes horse races. My mood was erratic, the future uncertain, even more so than when I left Seattle in January.

◆   ◆   ◆

I had a reprieve from Tipton. I was driving to Chicago to pick up daughter Nellie, who was flying in from Seattle. Nellie, majoring in fine art and French literature at the University of Washington, wanted to visit the Art Institute. I did too since the museum had Grant Wood's "American Gothic" in its permanent collection. This painting is one of the most famous things to come out of Iowa, maybe the most famous with the exception of bratwurst and bacon.

At loose ends, I cycled a few miles into the country west of town. Later, I ate a frugal breakfast at the Cove and read an old NYT. I walked for another look at the spot where my third grade country school had been. After it stopped being a school, the little building was used to store corn and then became a hog house before it was torn down to make way for a factory that made RV accessories. For some reason I remembered taking part in a wartime rubber collection drive, the slogan of which was "Slap the Japs with your rubber scraps!"

I wonder if I will be as nostalgic about my time here in 1988 as I am about my boyhood memories of being a farm kid in 1945? I think not. I'll have some 1988 snapshot memories of Christine and talks at her kitchen table, and being amused by Ginny and Bridget. Some nice recollections of drinking beer with Conn before he went home to Dublin. The Tipton library was pleasant. Bicycle rides in the country. Quiet loneliness blended with serenity.

◆   ◆   ◆

My attitude was a mix of introspection and bravado. I was eager for change. I had serious doubts about the wisdom of staying in Iowa. I missed the West but exactly what I missed was hard to pin down. I engaged in melodrama. I compared my time in Tipton to an unfinished sonata. Not a symphony. Too extravagant. Something of limited length and ambition, but nevertheless important and beautiful.

Ruby's old mansion sometimes was alight, under new management and busy with guests. I recalled the big single malt whiskey party we had there in April, when Christine became very drunk, and passed out very becomingly. On these evenings, the later it got and the more I walked the more morose I became. I had a sinking feeling of accomplishing nothing, leaving no mark in Cedar County except for a few clownish antics and those little evergreens Christine and I planted along the mansion's driveway. I had the Maid-Rite memories, the bicycle rides on gorgeous spring mornings before the crops began to die and blow away. To pass the time, I wrote exaggerated and overheated letters.

To Carol: "A typical morning here, more or less. I crawled out at 7:30, forgot to do my five minutes of exercise, didn't take a shower because I didn't want to interfere with the healing of the crater on my forehead (skin cancer surgery). I got dressed in L.L. Bean clothes and walked over to the Maid-Rite, going by the alley rather than the cornfield. I ordered black coffee with a plain cake doughnut and read the *Des Moines Register* cover to cover. It was brimming with stories about sports and the need for more economic development in Iowa and the endless dangers of a declining population. A state full of old people.

"I cycled to the p.o. where I found a letter from my convict brother. He wrote he had periods of sadness but was coping and making plans for his eventual release. He enjoyed the day he went to court in Salt Lake for his divorce hearing. Bill was in chains head to foot and when the prison guards waltzed him through the jail on the way to the courtroom the jail inmates parted "like the Red Sea" to let him pass. Bill enjoyed the moment.

"Otherwise, not much at the post office except the telephone bill, surprisingly low, only $27.86, in spite of lots of credit card calls from places like Glenview, Illinois, and Barstow, California. A Van Gogh postcard from Ken who was in Sausalito, remembering the days we cycled across the Golden Gate on Sunday mornings on our way to breakfast on Bridgeway, back when the world was younger and both of us assumed we had a future. It turned out we did have a future, probably better than the ones we imagined.

"I am nervous about leaving Iowa because it is familiar and cheap. I am being sentimental. Not much for me here and it is time to start drifting westward. I do need some time to tie up loose ends, including helping my folks straighten out some problems associated with old age and infirmities. I also should try harder to wind up my Cedar County journal. Sometimes I think of opening lines for a Cedar County memoir.

"For instance, I thought about calling this story something like: 'The story of Jake, a man who couldn't make up his mind if he should be Cedar County Jake or Yellowstone Jake.' Or: 'During the spring of '45, I walked to a one-room school house down the gravel road from our two-barn farm in Cedar County and wondered what I would do if Adolf Hitler came along in a car and offered me a ride.'

◆   ◆   ◆

Luckily for my emotional well being, Nellie and I got in the Rabbit late in August after Chicago visit and drove east, for an interlude at South Fallsburg, New York, with Carol, her daughter and mother at a Hindu ashram (of all places). I spent most of my time in the "honey hut" drinking unusually good coffee and watching people.

During the ride to South Fallsburg, Nellie made two memorable comments. One was that she thought people in Iowa lived in the past. And, on a rainy morning on New York Route 17, while gazing at dripping trees and landscape sliding past, Nellie said the scene reminded her of a Watteau painting she had seen in Paris. Her comment convinced me she was getting a lot out of her middle-class liberal arts education.

On to Newport, Rhode Island, to read a few epitaphs in very old cemeteries and spend some time with Ken who was living in Newport between marriages. We looked at Ivy League tans and profiles and ate well in seafood restaurants. Nellie and I wound up in Pennsylvania Station and a few days of Manhattan life. After that, well, for me, it was back west with a stop in Worcester, Mass., for a couple of days with friends drinking a little whiskey and moving on back toward Snotpit to face the music of the rest of my life.

◆   ◆   ◆

Before I got back to Cedar County, I woke up in a Motel 6 outside Youngstown, Ohio, took a long look at my room, thought about the 600 or so miles I would drive that day and admitted I was tired of the driving life. Maybe it was true the more you drove the dumber you got. That day's drive turned out to total 612 miles, mostly automatic except for the usual frenzied aspects of the section on Interstate 80 south of Chicago. I came off the freeway that night, turning north at the Tipton exit (Iowa 38) stunned and numbed at the same time. A moment or two of panic when I thought I had no more excuses about making a decision on what to do next. Was I ever going to finish my Cedar County memoir? I came up with an excuse which pleased me. Wanting to put off real life as long as possible, Carol and I made plans to spend some time on the Big Island of Hawaii in October. My next L.A. run on the Grey Dog was only a month away.

I told myself I was lonely but not pathetic and took long bicycle rides in the country trying to revive romantic Grant Wood notions of Iowa regionalism and the rightness of appreciating where you came from. My impression was I was more tired after these rides than inspired, although the countryside always looked like home. I switched to Pabst Blue Ribbon because it was a nickel or two cheaper than Old Style, and spent more time looking for aluminum cans worth a nickel refund.

I enjoyed more visits to Ruby's grave where my monologue described the summer and my drifting day dreams. Relax, I told myself, the world once was my oyster and could be again. I read cheap novels and went to bed at 9:30. I had coffee with Stu Clark who said crop yields were down remarkably but a combination of higher prices triggered by scarcity and government help meant most farmers were not hurting too much. Killing time. What I needed was an injection of the "patience and poise" the female guru talked about relentlessly at the S. Fallsburg ashram. She preached "patience and poise" while slowly waving her big peacock fan in the direction of the rapt audience.

I wrote Conn in Ireland, trying for perspective but lapsing into pessimism. "Your question of the summer remains unanswered. Why don't Tipton kids go to Iowa City and get into some heavy drugs and sex instead of driving around ceaselessly on Saturday night? They are still cruising with more dedication than ever.

"Today it's raining. First moisture in weeks. The drought is bad but nobody seems terribly upset. It is hard to get much emotion out of these Germanic people. I have been to the North Star Lounge a few times, once with Christine. Your spirit was hunched at the end of the bar, your back to the TV, pouring down Old Milwaukee. I suppose by now you have been laid numerous times, eliminating the memory of the Tipton dry spell, your prisoner of war experience in a wasteland of the pleasures of the flesh. After you left, there was nobody to drink beer with on a regular basis."

Conn didn't answer. No surprise.

◆   ◆   ◆

The Maid-Rite didn't let me down. I went in at 11 on a Sunday morning. Mostly silence from the church-goers dropping in after services. One young man was talking about football at Iowa State. His reverent tone probably was similar to the sermon he had just left. An older man talked soberly about an radio interview with the head football coach at the University of Northern Iowa. Two old folks sat chewing contentedly. An elderly woman stared into the near distance. She resembled a bulldog or a bull snake. Conversationally, the scene was like the reptile house at a zoo. Iowans are instinctively conservative of energy. Not unfriendly, necessarily, or cold, because occasionally one will look at his or her companion with a look that is somewhat friendly. Attention, though, is centered on the job at hand. Reading the menu, chewing or paying the check.

◆   ◆   ◆

I dithered, worried about things like self respect and dignity. Walking around town I got the feeling people were staring at me because they didn't understand what I was doing in their town. Maybe they disliked me because I seemed indolent and useless in a society based on the work ethic. I solved the problem by walking at night. Then I decided people also stared at me after dark. I solved the problem by staying in alleys during my nighttime strolls.

One afternoon in mid-September I glanced out my big window and leaves were falling from the elm across the street.

◆   ◆   ◆

Tipton and I began to disengage. I started living instead of observing. I relaxed but my life did not change much from the way it had been since Conn left and Christine moved away. I didn't handle loneliness any better and tended to feel a mounting sense of unease when I thought of the future. A walk at the Rochester Cemetery was calming. The oaks were barely beginning to turn. I stopped at the Cove for a cup of mud and a piece of apple pie.

◆   ◆   ◆

One evening in my kitchen I felt a rush of well being. I realized that after an hour or two at the library reading John McPhee in the *New Yorker* I could come home and eat ice cream and sliced bananas. On such prosaic rewards I ran my life.

By October, the nights were turning colder, into the low 20s. One afternoon, after a day in Iowa City, as I drove back to Tipton I accepted for the first time that as much as I enjoyed aspects of Iowa, I didn't belong anymore. It was not 1945, and I was not a farm kid. I was a displaced person. I was a lingerer, a watcher, and I didn't feel right in a spectator role. Maybe it was time to try harder to be happy. An old friend from Iowa City, long moved away, said Midwesterners were not comfortable with the thought of being happy. They had always been told happiness was not part of the scheme. Like Turgenev, who wrote that when it came to happiness he was an atheist.

◆   ◆   ◆

Time came to saddle up, and I was gone on the last of the '88 escapes, this time to Los Angeles and Hawaii. The way west, the plains across, Rockies, Colorado Plateau, angling southwest to Las Vegas through the Virgin River Canyon, breakfast in Barstow, the run west on the San Berdoo Freeway. Carol and the Chrysler at 6th and Los Angeles.

17

I grinned when I got off the Greyhound at the Iowa City station. I breathed deeply of the cold fresh air and turned up College Street to begin the walk across the river to my folk's place. It was early November and nippy. The trees were almost leafless, getting into their black winter garb. Autumn had come and gone and I was sorry.

Carol had cried at the bus station before I headed for Gate 9, the New York bus via Denver. On the way out of Los Angeles at 7th and Alameda, I saw a sign on a warehouse that said: "L.A. Nuthouse." I smiled and nodded. By Claremont, I was on the road again, white line fever, looking forward to the lunch stop at Barstow.

We ran into snow the other side of Vail, Colorado, but otherwise the long ride was unmarked by much to remember. One exception was that while crossing the plains east of Sterling, Colorado, our path hit a squall line which was fun to watch develop into wind, rain and a few minutes of semi-darkness. I did wonder while gazing at the Colorado Plateau if I had been a prairie dog in a previous life. The country looked so familiar.

My only insight during the Iowa City-Los Angeles-Hawaii run (except for a new appreciation for Kona coffee) was that I was partial to what I now called "the real West." This reference meant I had repudiated the distasteful urban coastal West of smog, blight, congestion, grubby materialism and high prices. I embraced a clean ideal of the rural West, an area I learned was known as "the interior West." Vaguely defined as east of Barstow, and west of the Rockies. An absence of people meant fewer annoyances but you still had the grand and inspiring scenery. I agreed with Hemingway's comment that "the only thing that could spoil a day was people" except, as he added, "for the very few who were as good as spring itself."

In my new utopian mood, I recalled a conversation years before with Hawaii's Lt. Gov. Tom Gill in his office at Iolani Palace. He said people who lived in pollution and blight were like goldfish in a fishbowl where no one ever changed the water. "Eventually, one day all the fish died. The change to toxicity was go gradual and so insidious the goldfish never knew they were sick."

◆   ◆   ◆

Tipton was no surprise. The same gray, bleak, cold scene I had seen in my mind's eye and sometimes longed for during hot toxic Los Angeles afternoons. A stinging wind out of the northwest invigorated me as I walked back from the post office. No mail of any importance. I warmed up to my self-assigned job of writing my Cedar County memoir, and then getting out, to fulfill my greater mission of finishing my dad's life for him.

◆   ◆   ◆

Warm up time. To Q in Amherst:

"I have been living Yeat's line about making a choice between the life and the art. I have chosen the former because that is where the fun and the travel and the women are. Earlier, in July, I went to Nevada with an old friend so she could revisit copper pits of her youth. We are talking of living together in Los Angeles. I am tepid about Los Angeles for a variety of reasons, all of them banal and predictable but still powerful. Carol, however, represents a chance for happiness. You see my dilemma.

"In a perverse way, I enjoy the bleakness and the cold and the economy of line I see in rural Iowa. The people, though, many of them, resemble reptiles. They show cold-blooded ways of conserving energy, particularly intellectual and conversational energy. A crocodile can get by on a couple of big meals a year. The people around here could survive on half a dozen football games, an Iowa win in the NCAA tourney, a couple of good divorces to talk about and a morning of closet cleaning.

"It is a lonely and isolated life which might be tolerable if I were less in need of talking to people once in a while. But I do find solace in the solitude. I like the way the horizon looks, open and clear. Even so, I sympathize with a friend who lives in smoggy Pasadena. He wrote me that he is developing a cough and knows it is unhealthy where he lives. 'But I'm 66 years old and where else will I find old friends and the cultural life I enjoy so much? I could move away to a healthier environment but who would I go to lunch with?'"

"Who can say? One of life's hardest question is how to live it.

"I also am nervous about the Southern California approach of guru-swami self-realization. I am not a believer. I don't think exercise makes you rich or that crystals make a brain tumor disappear. I admit there are laws we know nothing of, but I'm suspicious of people who have discovered life's secrets and will pass them on, for a finder's fee.

"Urban places sometimes fill me with dread. I don't like the air, the traffic, the human swarm, the passing lane mentality, the high costs, the sense of having to be on your guard. That doesn't leave much to like since I can live without most trappings of culture such as art museums, symphony orchestras, expensive restaurants and non-fat yogurt shops."

I could afford this luxury of anti-urban feelings. Cities were where the jobs were for people like me. I didn't need one, at the moment.

◆   ◆   ◆

I picked up my summer routine except for the vanished life at Victorian House. I left the Maid-Rite one morning in a light snowfall. On the way back to the bunker I found 15 cents worth of beer cans. The wind was howling and the view to the north was a flattened soybean field, looking exactly the same as when I came in February. I admitted a deep reservoir of affection for Iowa, the place. I enjoyed the weather, chilly and changeable, especially since I no longer worked outside. The winter landscape appealed to something equally bleak and thrifty in my personality, all gray and angular and quiet.

◆   ◆   ◆

Ken was one of my oldest friends. I met him when I was 14, on the firing range in the basement at Iowa City High School. We were both freshman and trying out for the rifle team. I owned him a lot over the years. He and his pal Quentin introduced me to English movies and sardonic humor as well as the fun of occasional arrogance and elitism. I was best man at Ken's first wedding (the first of several). After his first divorce, we went to San Francisco together at the tail end of the beatnik era. We lived in a little apartment on Page Street off Market under the 101 Freeway. We were copy boys at a newspaper that disappeared years ago. We got up at 4 a.m. and rode our bicycles down dark and wet Market Street along the slippery streetcar tracks to work the early shift. Eventually, he settled in New England. We kept in touch.

One afternoon a couple of years ago as he and I drove through Pennsylvania toward Iowa, we talked about why it was that he had moved East and I stayed in the West. We had each lived a while on both coasts. We decided our different preferences were based partly on accidents and partly on family histories. I had my dreamy dad and western movies; he had summers in Maine and an eastern twist to his family ties.

We saw each other frequently, often in Iowa. A main reason for our continuing connection was a shared fondness, tenderness even, for Iowa City and luxuriant memories of our life there. When we met in Iowa City, we sat next to the sidewalk window at The Airliner bar on South Clinton Street across from the campus, as much at ease with our environment and each other as if we were still high school sophomores deciding what to do that night.

Toward the end of my Iowa interlude, I wrote him.

"I have mixed feelings. I am aware it is time to move on. Even so, I have not lost my deep affection for Iowa. I can't say the people have changed much, at least in the rural environs where I hang out. I guess I am generalizing but I feel a coziness that does not wear well. Especially, I am still liking Iowa City. I suppose I recall fondly the days when you lived there, and Quentin was still alive, the old gang before marriage and death and re-marriage and moving away. Days of pre-marital simplicity. I go to Iowa City now, hit the Hamburg Inn No. 2 and read the NYT, have a beer at George's, drink coffee and read at the bagel place, browse at book stores, visit the university library and check out books with my non-student borrower's permit.

"Sometimes I walk in Oakland Cemetery, a fine place to think, and spy out old friends and relatives who now live there permanently. Quentin and Wendell, my grandparents and your dad. Sometimes I stop by Virgil Hancher's grave and chat. He would never talk to me when he was president of the university and I was an annoying reporter at the *Daily Iowan*.

"Tipton, in contrast, has advantages of cheapness and distance from distractions. My income-producing future is uncertain. I can last a while longer, even in Los Angeles, on my investments. The day is coming, though, when I will start selling stock, and it is dangerous to erode one's capital. I'll worry about it tomorrow."

◆   ◆   ◆

My days, and usually nights, were spent mining my journals and computer storage for fair-to-middling Cedar County nuggets. I lived inside myself, and had to find little rewards. A third cup of coffee, a second can of beer, an evening or afternoon walk to the library to read the *New Yorker*, a movie or meal with my folks. At night, I walked past Victorian House and looked at the white wicker furniture still on the porch.

Carol called one evening and said she was a little skittish about living with me. She had concerns about my ambiguous future, and Jack Benny cheap-ass attitudes about money. Jack Benny and I both considered money to be paper blood. My loner mentality bothered her as well as my obvious lack of enthusiasm regarding Southern California. She wanted to try being more independent of men (I was skeptical of this one). Some of these subjects had surfaced already during a memorable late night dispute on the Santa Monica Freeway that generated a lot of heat and very little light. I had disgraced myself by displaying too much stridency and not enough calm coherence. Waking up late at night, I peeked over the edge of the canyon of old age and loneliness. A man with a penchant for missing the brass ring.

◆   ◆   ◆

A letter arrived from a publisher saying two readers liked my work on the Manhattan Project's plutonium works and the manuscript would be read by a third for further evaluation. I repainted my VW's bumpers flat black for the second time in four months. I had a spirited conversation with my folks about using gasoline as a paint brush cleaner. I became obsessed with dental hygiene and every morning before the Maid-Rite and nightly before retiring I scraped my tongue with a stainless steel spoon, flossed, brushed, gargled with Listerine.

The Maid-Rite got a laugh. A man came in, some friends yelled at him to sit with them. "Aw, I smell like hogs."

"That's okay," they said, "We're used to it."

With my new and personally distressing negativity about much of the West, and Carol talking about snatching away my shelter in Los Angeles, I began to look for another way. I wrote Dr. Dick in Portland and told him I was ready when he was if new travel ideas came up in his pursuit of locales for his next novel. My passport was valid and American Express was paid in full. Maybe, he said, Borneo for cannibalism; Egypt for a Sphinx-based mystery; Berlin for the Wall.

During a late walk, road visions of the Four Corners swept suddenly into my thoughts, like stray neutrons igniting a uranium pile. I began to heat up about Colorado's Western Slope. A professor friend had written with advice that there might be a story there about a society he called "the uranium culture." He wrote about going to Naturita, Colorado, "talking to Peyote Coyote and Red Cedar Woman, good stories, Studs Terkel stuff. It's another world, and I think you would like it. You can escape into the mountains and hot springs at Ouray or bars at Silverton fairly quickly. I guess I'm a little homesick."

A call from Kim in Washington, D.C. She was my Sioux Indian ex-sweetie. Kim said she might be heading for Colorado's Western Slope in late winter to live on unemployment. "It's nice, those mountain towns, really interesting people, and I owe you for Seattle." Her uncle had been a uranium geologist on the Colorado Plateau during the glory days of exploration and discovery, the Charlie Steen era of million-dollar uranium finds.

Funny, the little things you pick up from friends. Christine taught me the delights of cole slaw with walnuts. Kim, who called herself an Indian princess, my Indian princess, showed me how to mix black beans and brown rice and add Frank's RedHot cayenne pepper sauce.

Sometimes, to remind me of the world out there, I had a beer or two, put Lacy J. Dalton on the tape player, and danced clumsily, laughing, singing along, "another B grade movie for life's big silver screen."

◆   ◆   ◆

Sunday morning, 11 December 1988: Up at 8, reluctantly because the room was cold. Breakfast of whole wheat toast, papaya-pineapple jam from Kamuela, Uncle Sam cereal with flaxseed from Omaha, and a banana. A bit of reading. I listened to a Czech string quartet for a while on St. Paul Sunday Morning broadcast by KSUI in Iowa City followed by a cold walk to the Maid-Rite to read yesterday's *New York Times* and write Xmas cards. To the p.o. to mail the cards, and a roundabout walk back to the bunker, my face stinging with cold. I went out of my way to check on a yard where I had seen an empty Mountain Dew can worth five cents. I thought about the future, my future, social and sexual and financial and otherwise, and decided to finish the autobiographical fragment very soon, and hope that Carol could visit and after that take the Greyhound to Florida to see the other Carol for a week or two. After that, my life was open, except for a possible sojourn in Los Angeles followed by a stab at the uranium culture in the Four Corners or to Borneo or Queensland or drinking beer along the River Spree in East Berlin with Dr. Dick. Back to the bunker to listen to loud Grieg on KSUI, Piano Concerto in A Minor Opus 16, Radio Symphony Orechestra of Berlin. The piece was vividly evocative of a Norwegian coastal steamer trip from Bergen to Alesund. Blue fjords and ripe wheat fields and majestic mountains. I cooked a pot of whole grain brown organic rice to go with black beans and raw green pepper for lunch, wrote more holiday notes and read a little, with an occasional foray into journal writing. I couldn't help but notice how my mood improved after a walk during which I had a few daydreams and made a few tentative decisions. In addition, I had a movie to look forward to that evening at the Hardacre. I was told the Hardacre was the last picture show in all of Cedar County. Sometimes I liked my life in Cedar County but my dream life was farther on, somewhere west of North Platte.

◆   ◆   ◆

On the last day of 1988, I walked down Lynn Street south of the bunker and turned right on an icy cross street to an open space where I could watch the sun go down. A great orange orb was sinking behind what passed for a horizon. In the near foreground were a small, rust-pitted pickup, and two small white frame houses. Farther away, a jagged line of small trees and one big tree, leafless and black and spooky. Back at the bunker, I shot the sunset with an Old Style, raising the can in a toast: "To the last of the light."

I spoke to Carol who said it was raining in Los Angeles.

18

I lingered into the new year. Mild, dry and mid-winter. The biggest change in daily life occurred when Kay and Wally at the Maid-Rite broke tradition by not opening until 9 a.m. six days a week. They closed on Sunday. Suddenly, the day had a different look. Before the sea change in Maid-Rite hours, awake in the dark mid-watch of the night, I found comfort knowing the place would open at 5 a.m. I desperately missed the Maid-Rite diversion on Sundays, with the mix of the churched and unchurched, saved and unsaved. Tipton became as dead as England's suicidal Sundays. If I wanted human presence I drove nine miles south to the Cove on I-80. For me, the Cove lacked Maid-Rite intimacy.

Soon after the year began, Lee and Deidre, the young managers at Victorian House, left Tipton to seek a future in Colorado Springs. I had become attached to them and their inexpensive good lunches of chicken salad and cole slaw. The Gelms, by then entrenched in their new place in Bellevue along the Mississippi, quietly put the Tipton mansion on the market. At night, when I walked by, the towered house was dark, and belonged again to Ruby.

I heard my first really ugly racist remark at the Maid-Rite, a day or two before the Martin Luther King holiday. A young man told his booth mates, in full voice heard throughout the café, that he never thought he would get a paid day off "because of some nigger's birthday."

◆　　　◆　　　◆

My emotional bags were packed, but I dawdled and waited for a sign. Of course, I wondered: What had the months in this little town

183

proved? Had the experience changed me? Moved me? I wasn't really able to say, at least not able to say anything weighty or moving. I waited for ethereal ideas of the epilogue variety, but all I could think of were commonplace notions. Such as: I learned little things from Christine. I hated it now when people poisoned old Victorian houses with concrete steps and wrought iron porch railings, and I really liked walnuts in cole slaw.

I thought, well, really, in summation. Maid-Rite days. Victorian summer. Winter dreams.

My thoughts were random, shaped by loneliness and the knowledge I would be leaving soon, long before spring. Tipton had been where I lived, maybe not always with enthusiasm but I got my mail there. With winter Tipton became a place I was staying in, while preparing my ship for sea. I tuned in the Quad Squad to check how the d.j. with the M.A. was doing at the mike, and heard: It's Bob Gelms, live at the Burger King!

While walking on the east side of courthouse square at dusk, a willowy, dark-haired woman in a hooded coat walked rapidly past me with a friendly nod. If I knew her, maybe Tipton wouldn't be so cold and I wouldn't feel so isolated. Another day I watched a long-haired redhead wearing a heavy dark coat and floppy tennis shoes over heavy socks walk across the icy trailer park driveway to the line of mailboxes. She walked back to her trailer where the screen door was swinging in the southeast wind. I thought, there, buddy, is a story, could be a story. Forget these solitary musings, I told myself. Life is the teacher; get to it.

◆   ◆   ◆

When I felt critical of Tipton I remembered tape-recorded conversations with people who did not want their names used.

"It seems to me that people who live here are people who don't have the drive or the ambition or whatever to go out and reach their full potential and experience what the world has to offer. These are people quite content to marry young, and settle here, live close to mom and dad, get a job, not a career, and make enough money to have a house. That's the first thing buy before you get married. You have enough time to go out with your friends on Friday night, for softball, volley-ball, basketball, bowling, and that's life. I can see a draw to that, where it would be comfortable and a relatively relaxed lifestyle. The extended family is good too. But it's a model for living I have never subscribed to. I find it hard to understand, which just says I am not a small town person."

And: "Well, yes, I think a lot of people here have, what shall I call it? A low level of mentality."

On reflection, I decided I might buy these generalizations but only if many exceptions were noted. For instance, people like Sheriff Whit-latch, the implement dealer Jacobsen, Stu Clark, Bob and Christine, Krob & Esbeck, Mary Jane Huber, Christine's "old fossil" Martha Jane Henry, landlord Ken Muller, city manager Snavely.

◆   ◆   ◆

Always for me, there was something about Iowa, something about a low horizon, a cramped feeling, negative and nagging. Talking one afternoon to Lee and Deidre in the dining room, Deidre nailed what was gnawing at me. I asked her why they were leaving for Colorado. She listed the usual reasons, including more opportunity in their field of hotels and restaurants, brighter lights, glamour, newness. I asked her to express her feelings about Iowa in one phrase.

"Hokey. Iowa's hokey," said Deidre, who had spent part of her young life growing up in Santa Ana, Calif. She was tired of her friends from other states making jokes about Iowa hayseeds and getting Iowa confused with Idaho. "My California friends can't even pronounce Iowa. They say "a-Wa or O-wa." She was right. Most people thought it was the sticks, full of rubes, people with a bad case of the slows. A friend at the Associated Press in San Francisco, a New Yorker, railed at me one night because I wasn't getting stories on the wire fast enough to suit him. "You can take the boy out of Iowa but you can't take Iowa out of the boy," he yelled.

◆   ◆   ◆

I knew, though, even as a boy, that Iowa was not nearly as backward or as crowded with hayseeds as non-Iowans liked to think it was. Even so, as a callow youth, I was impressed easily by other states, usually for half-formed reasons connected to spurious but powerful images from movies or books. For instance, Illinois was interesting because it was more populous and Chicago was there. St. Valentine's Day Massacre, Al Capone, Sandburg's "City of the Big Shoulders." Illinois also had Rock Island, East Moline and East Dubuque, all familiar across the Mississippi and all rumored to contain whorehouses and gangsters. Vice was exciting and didn't exist in Iowa.

Missouri possessed a southern character which meant the romance of the Lost Cause of the Confederacy. St. Louis had jazz and Negroes and professional baseball. Kansas City had a cow town past. Most of all, Missouri was associated with Tom Sawyer and Huck Finn and, in Iowa, you couldn't get more literary than Mark Twain.

Nebraska was where the west began. (Later in life, I pinpointed the spot a mile west of the I-80 exit to Gothenburg, Nebraska. In the near distance, you can see the beginnings of rocky ridges and endless vistas of aridity.) The Plains Indians, the most glamourous of all, roamed and fought and hunted buffalo in Nebraska. The Oregon/California and Mormon trails followed the Platte.

Minnesota didn't offer much, since my stereotyping occurred before Minneapolis-St. Paul became an acceptable urban area, thanks to Garrison Keillor. Minnesota and Iowa, for me as a boy, were pretty much a horse apiece. The northern neighbor was a colder and bleaker extension of home. Wisconsin was bosky and progressive and reportedly pretty but its dairy farm reputation was a hick drawback.

The Dakotas except for dad's stories of wandering and harvest work were unfamiliar, although I knew my dad's great-uncle had left Iowa for the Dakota prairies. I was aware Wild Bill Hickok, an icon of western movie culture, was shot dead in Deadwood, S.D. Other western states like Wyoming, Montana, New Mexico and Arizona, also were unmapped country except, again, for dad's stories of harvests and westward adventuring. Idaho was not in the running because many people confused it with Iowa.

The coastal west meant California and California was and is, for me, the Land o' Dreams. In those days I had no idea of the geographical complexity of Oregon and Washington. When we lived in Washington in '43, wartime gas rationing kept us close to home most of the time.

South meant Texas. Iowans went there in the winter and came back with negative impressions, mostly because of the suffocating humidity of the Gulf Coast.

Almost any place east was exotic, with the exception of Ohio and Indiana. These states shared Iowa's lack of edge, although Ohio was noted for heavy industry and, in those days, Cleveland was a robust city. Years later, I was a reporter in Ohio and realized it had a lot more going for it than I had realized in my benighted youth. Indiana held two symbols of allure to a typical Iowa hick: the Indy 500, and Notre Dame, which in those days was the gold standard in college football romance. Michigan did nothing for me except for a juvenile admiration of its athletic program and the fact that Detroit was where cars came from.

Iowa was in the middle, the butt of jokes. Iowa was not on the border of anything. It was the sticks, insulated from change and trends which coastal areas enjoyed. Since it was in the middle, there was no shortage of escapist destinations for the talented and restless. The ones who stayed apparently wanted to stay, a condition which contributed to a lack of creative tension. Again, these were examples of my juvenile perceptions, and later, with the help of worldly experience, to be discarded.

Like most places, Iowa's climate was less than ideal, although often it would surprise with a dry cool July day and a warm sunny February afternoon. Generally, the stereotype was true though. Bone-chilling cold and smothering humidity. Rare was the day you could leave doors and windows open or when people could sit in their front yard or lounge on un-screened porches without either freezing or suffocating or being eaten alive by tiny things that flew or crawled.

To my immature eyes, the landscape was boring. It tended to flatness and seemed void of features. In college, I often quoted Herodotus who said somewhere that "flat lands breed flat men." Later, I realized "undulating" was a better description. When I thought Iowa was flat I had never seen Kansas or Texas.

Not much that was famous came from Iowa except anti-glamour commodities like corn and hogs. No doubt the ecstasy which greeted successes of the university's athletes was grounded in the excitement of being known coast to coast for something other than bacon and rural virtues. People might say, "Oh, yeah, the team that went into double overtime with UCLA."

After I grew up, I realized it was good to be in a state that had few tourist attractions, a quiet place where phoniness and ostentation were avoided and plain speaking was appreciated. Even if the air was frigid or humidly oppressive, it was breathable.

On my second time around, as a Tiptonian, less narrow minded and inexperienced, I admired another attribute of Iowans, at least farmers and rural folks. I appreciated their bedrock pragmatism. I heard it expressed every day at the Maid-Rite when the customers talked politics or pesticides. I liked their no-nonsense linear nature.

A writer in the Washington Post, Joel Garreau, described this attitude. "The minority which actually farms knows the truth of that old barnyard expression: you can't bullshit a cow. You can't pull the stunts of language, faking it, that can be so much a part of working in an office or on an assembly line. You get that cow food and water and medicine and you get her the hell out of the wind and snow or she dies. Thud!"

♦   ♦   ♦

Feeling myself slipping away, I wrote to my friend who had moved with his family to Lima, Peru. "My cash reserve is down to $5,000, not counting comfortable investments (sort of a joke). I don't owe any money, except a continuing obligation to get daughter Nellie through college. She's a senior at the University of Washington but she may want to get a double major in fine art and French literature which would mean an extra semester or two. I don't mind. Her education is one of the things in my life that is working out well.

"The memoir, well, heaven knows what will become of it. Maybe a private publication. I have thought, in antic moments, of calling it the *Snotpit Chronicle*. It started as a fairly serious oral history then took a sudden turn after I met Christine to personal odyssey/comedy/angst. I will leave, I think, with a heavy heart, not because I want to stay but because I have not accomplished what I set out to do. Ideally, I wanted to write an elegiac account of coming home. Probably, Cedar County had not changed much. I had. No longer a farm kid.

"My folks, in memory so vital and vigorous, had changed too. My mother, such a worker and resolute person, is frail and short of breath. My dad, once so strong and resourceful, has become mixed up to the point where he can't drive a car or remember what Christmas is about. He puts orange juice on his breakfast food and cottage cheese on toast and shaves with toothpaste. He waves to people he sees on television.

"In Garrison Keillor's last book he said we all will cry the same tears as our ancestors. Life is a hard road; everybody must walk it. Personally, I think some people ride at least part of the way.

"I went to a grave side service Tuesday morning for the mother of an old friend. The minister (Church of Good News) read a little from Job and the burial service. He said funerals were not for the dead but for the living. They were to remind us how far we had to go and what we had to do on the way. This service was on a snowy hillside of a country cemetery where I had worked when in high school mowing grass and digging graves. Within sight of Tuesday's burial was the grave of a friend of mine from sixth grade who died of an abscessed tooth. The wind was penetrating and the mourners shivered uncontrollably. I listened to what the minister was saying and I thought what he said was true. I thought of my friend's mother, whose ashes were in a tiny black box next to my feet, and how she had lived alone for years after her husband ran off. She died midway between the telephone and her kitchen three days before Christmas, apparently after exhausting herself with last minute shopping.

"That's about the size of it. Time for lentil soup and brown rice, maybe a slice or two of raw green pepper and an Old Style, a snatch of classical music, a bit of reading, then "to revel in the pleasures of an unshared bed."

◆   ◆   ◆

After January, plans changed. Things jelled. Carol came from California to Iowa, to the bunker, for 10 days. She waltzed through the arrival gate at the Cedar Rapids airport wearing flashy multi-colored cowboy boots and a majestic fur coat that had belonged to her grandmother. She was a great-looking eccentric with kinky dark red hair and the stage presence of an actress in her prime. After a few days of Iowa life, which meant eating out and going to bed early, she lifted her ban on my living with her. A little after the first of March I will be headed west to make a new beginning. No such thing as a new life at my age. Our life-changing conversation occurred in the space between the word processor and the bed early one afternoon.

"What about the future?" I asked.

"Come to L.A.": she replied.

"And do what?"

"Live with me."

◆   ◆   ◆

My anxiety level about this change of life was fairly high. The bottom line was that Carol was worth the risk of madness. Until we had our summit meeting next to the Kaypro, I was beginning to wonder where I would go. I knew I would leave Cedar County, but didn't know exactly where to go. Somewhere west. I had mixed feelings about leaving Iowa, partly because of my parents' aged condition. I realized this year had been unusual for them and for me and would not be repeated. Truth is a hard apple. At a certain age time becomes uncomfortably measurable.

To myself I admitted this particular move was a difficult one, more so than most I had made in a life of moving on. I anticipated a good beginning with Carol but at the same time suffered from a sadness laced with nostalgia. I had had a good year. Going back to California did not carry the thrill it did in '59 or '61 or all those other times I returned for a while. And, I guess a lot of the San Francisco bias against Southern California that had shaped me in my formative years lingered, although for a long time I had been curious about Los Angeles either as a place to live or as a place to go to seed.

◆   ◆   ◆

I was looking for a literary hook for my feelings about Iowa. A friend suggested reading Wallace Stegner's *Wolf Willow*, a memoir of his small town boyhood in Saskatchewan. I scanned the book, looking for insight. Maybe it's tacky to take another man's writing to express oneself, but I didn't see how I or anyone could have written it better. His hometown, he wrote, was "as good a place to be a boy and as unsatisfying a place to be a man as one could well imagine."

It was difficult, Stegner said, to describe his experiences there without either expressing "the scorn of a city intellectual or the angry defensiveness of a native son." Small and isolated towns provide two alternatives for talented and intelligent youth: frustration or escape. Still, Stegner maintained a deep affection for his hometown, although he thought few others would appreciate it, at least until more people were moved "by the beauty of the geometric earth and the enormous sky brimming with weather, and to learn the passion of loneliness and the mystery of the prairie wind."

Stegner was one of my favorite writers, and I never forgot the jacket blurb on his novel *Angle of Repose*, taken from a review in the *San Francisco Chronicle*. I thought it the truest jacket blurb I had ever read and itself a piece of literature:

"For when all is said, individual lives are very much like the bits of detritus, rolling down from the high places of stress and emotion until they reach that place where the tumbling and falling stops and they find their angle of repose."

◆   ◆   ◆

By the time I had returned to Iowa, tumbling and falling, I wasn't a farm boy or college student with my future all ahead of me. I wasn't dreaming of somewhere else, at first. I had come to stay a while. I thought I could live in Tipton and adjust and be happy at the Maid-Rite in the morning and the Hardacre on Friday nights. Maybe a stop or two during the week at the North Star. It worked for a while.

I had the same longings as before. I was after the same half-world of day dreams and immediate satisfactions I had always pursued. What I wanted was what Morley Callaghan described in his memoir called *That Summer in Paris*:

"Now that we were established we fell into a routine. We would get up around noon, walk slowly over to the Coupole, have a little lunch on the terrace, then go across the river to the American Express to inquire for mail. Sometimes we loafed around the Right Bank for two hours, having a drink at some café by the Opera, or the Madeleine, then making some purchase in the Galerie Lafayette, then go on to the Champs Elysees where the sunlight was on the trees."

◆　　◆　　◆

2/20/89. Saw Doc Krob at Maid-Rite. He recounted his recent trip to Sylmar (north of Los Angeles) during an unusual snowfall. Said it was pathetic, kids didn't know how to make snowballs. Later, in the evening, on walk back from stroll past Victorian House, I thought how slow I was to leave, because of the memory of the summer. You learn very little, I told myself, by asking questions. You learn in silence, by watching.

2/23/89. Eleven degrees tonight. No wind except for faint movement from south. So quiet in Snotpit on walk from bunker to library and back I met only one person. My footsteps were loud past the Hardacre. At Parson Sondrol's place a little breeze rustled the maple leaves. The sky was like the lines from *Ethan Frome*, the part about "a sky of iron, the points of the Dipper hung like icicles and Orion flashed his cold fires."

2/25/89. Saturday Maid-Rite morning. Four farmers, one with a bandaged thumb. They were talking about castrating hogs, like gutting or filleting a fish. One did a graphic demonstration with an imaginary scrotum and knife. They agreed it was devilishly hard to keep the knife sharp what with all that tough hog hide and wire-like hair.

◆　　◆　　◆

A heavy heart and dogged by loneliness. Feeling old and sad and nervous. Telling myself all is natural, closing a circle, as winter follows fall and leads to spring. No insights on what Tipton was except Victorian summer and winter dreams. Los Angeles frightening, that is true, but newness more so, although California is not new to me and neither was Carol. Anticipating new beginning but with eagerness laced with sadness and age.

◆   ◆   ◆

Financial update: credit union $3,600; stox $58,500; IRAs $12,800; cash $500; IRS refund $356; total $75,756. I had started with $16,860 in the credit union account, so had spent $13,260 in 13 months. I had lived well. Travel, beer, breakfast out. Lunch stops at Barstow, the S. Fallsburg ashram, Big Island, Major's Place. A full life, Chollie.

◆   ◆   ◆

2/26/89. Sunset on a cold day, and I am about to walk to the store to get beer to keep me company during my next to last night in Snot-pit. I am more emotional, I guess, about leaving than I ever thought. I had a good year any way you look at it. A renewal of my affection for this country, a Victorian summer with Christine and her girls, making the connection with Carol.

When you get right down to it what I am dreading about leaving is not the new beginning or Southern California or taking a chance on love. What bothers me is saying goodbye to the folks, realizing something has ended, followed by homesickness. I couldn't count the times I have driven from Iowa City to the coast, beginning in 1958 on the Greyhound to Oakland. When I think about it I had to wonder why? Such hesitation might mean I'm getting long in the tooth. I admit a sharp jolt when I think of the highway ahead, trucks and blowing snow, listening to engines, the throaty music, and down off the cold Wyoming plateau to Utah and Nevada deserts and driving into a Los Angeles spring. I don't think the hazy L.A. Basin is going to hit me as hard as seeing the San Francisco skyline across the Bay, rolling south into Berkeley in the days of U.S. 40, smelling the Bay, turning right on the Bay Bridge approach.

Let's face it, it was different then. I was 23, eyes wide and heart a-flutter, coming into San Francisco with Ken in the faded blue '49 Hudson, out of college and ready for life.

◆   ◆   ◆

I walked to the store on a starry night with snow underfoot. 21 degrees. Orion's cold fires burning. Uncanny sense of a cold and snow-covered night landscape. I walked back in my own version of *Ethan Frome* with a 40 oz. bottle of Pabst. I think during the first part of this entry I was experiencing semi-panic similar to what I felt before leaving Seattle. Cold and lonely. It's good, though, the way the unfamiliar becomes familiar. When I came to Snotpit, before I met Christine, at times I would feel myself beginning to assume an emotional fetal position. I was disoriented and uneasy. Now, about to depart, I have a comfortable routine. Of course, a lot of the fun of being here ended when the mad C. left my life.

2/27/89. This entry is the last before I pack the machinery. I'm down to two sheets of printer paper out of the 1,000 I brought with me a year ago. I've filed a change of address form at the p.o. The box rent expires tomorrow. The bunker is echoing with emptiness. I did make a last walk around town tonight. To the library to read the *Register* and *Conservative*, checked the magazines, ignored the books. A swing past Victorian House which was ablaze with light, a rare event in recent weeks. I guess the guy who lives there now wants to scare off the ghosts. On the way back to the bunker, I stopped at the North Star for an Old Style and to exchange a few words with Dick, the bartender who reminds ever so slightly of John Wayne. I remembered the early summer nights with Conn, the Irish degenerate. I imagined him slouching at the end of the bar working on an Old Milwaukee. Not much to say to Dick and I headed home. 22 degrees. Not really cold, and the stars were out. I remembered Major's Place and the limitless view of mountains, deserts and the star-filled heavens. I suppose from now on cold and starry nights will take me back to Tipton and the buried life.

No truths revealed. I guess the epiphanies will occur later, maybe in Big Tujunga Canyon or on the Santa Monica Freeway. In Seattle when I left I was giving up a life. Here, I am leaving behind something not really definable. A sojourn in a place where although I didn't really belong, I wasn't quite a stranger.

2/28/89. I packed the Kaypro and printer and stopped in at the Maid-Rite one last time. On the walk back I thought about being in Tipton for 13 months and having no one to write to after I left. Moved out of bunker and in with folks. Didn't look back and didn't drive past Victorian House.

3/1/89. Mother, thinking ahead, told me what to give Nellie when the time came. Promises to keep. Falling snow. Thinking of missed chances.

3/2/89. Off to the races tomorrow on I-80. Hometown blues.

3/3/89. 196,644 mileage on VW. Icy morning. Left for Nebraska against all advice. Made Lincoln and Lester and Lorna's place before dark, driving through sleet and freezing slush, the VW streaked with salt and road spray. I drove today in a haze. Hard to leave the folks but I felt a measure of relief. Iowa was wearing her winter dress of black and white with gray fog for lacing.

In Tipton I did achieve a certain happiness, eccentric perhaps. I knew, though, from the beginning, I would only be there for a while. My stay turned out to be a few months longer than I would have guessed. I think I figured being gone before Christmas. I will remember with pleasure the early summer. After that, life became mostly a round of Maid-Rite in the morning, a walk to the post office and library, more or less a reclusive lifestyle. I got some writing done, a couple of hundred pages of *Maid-Rite Days*, although here again I wonder how relevant what I wrote is to anything important. Yes, I wrote a little, had some fun, was lonely a lot, had good times with the folks, saw the corn come up, the snow come back. An affair of the heart that was ill-starred from the first day. An interlude in a familiar place, knowing from the first day I would be gone again. Not quite belonging, not quite a stranger.

3/4/89. Wyoming. The Antelope for supper east of Cheyenne on I-80. Hamburger steak and fried onions and lots of coffee to keep me awake until Cheyenne. Cowboys instead of farmers. Feels right to be headed west.

3/5/89. Motel 6 at Midvale, Utah, north of the state pen on I-15.

3/6/89. Visited Bill at the Big House. Reasonably good spirits. He's realistic and relaxed. He is thinking of going back to Iowa if he is paroled. Says he knows himself better than he did. Prison life does not frighten him anymore. He has some close friends and knows the routine.

3/7/89. Bill's last words after second visit: "You do the crime; you do the time."

3/8/89. Baker, Cal. I live in California now. Good easy fast ride from Utah. Before leaving Nevada I dined on taco salad at Whiskey Pete's Casino which is spitting distance from the California state line. I spent 10 minutes studying the bullet-holed Ford V8 sedan on exhibit in the casino lobby, the car Bonnie and Clyde died in. It turns out that Clyde Barrow liked Fords. He found them fast and reliable, excellent cars for the business he was in. I tipped my cap when I passed the California state line sign. A couple of beers at the Bun Boy bar in Baker. I called Carol in Sunland. She was excited., Me too.

Later

During the summer of 2002, I took the *Cedar County* manuscript out of storage and read parts of it. It read pretty well. I decided to try again to put it between the covers of a book. I spent some time working on it, adding and subtracting. I cut away the parts one reader described as having "a self-pitying tone."

When I completed the original version of *Cedar County* in 1990, I tried to interest commercial publishers, including university presses. No go. I photocopied about 35 copies. I sold them for $10 each, a profit of $1 since photocopying cost $9. The photocopies sparked some comment. Harold Romaine, my dad's boyhood friend from West Liberty, told me: "Better than Louis L'Amour." My mother's only comment: "Why so much sex?"

Other people, including an editor or two, had liked it, not because it was a great narrative but because of its personal qualities. One editor liked the manuscript a lot, and told me it was "painfully truthful in places, very funny in others, compelling and sympathetic and blunt in turn. I want to read all of it, but I know we can't publish it. It is too far out of the university press mold." She recommended I send it to the publisher of *Blue Highways*. I took her advice and was told the material "was not right for our present needs." This publisher suggested I find a literary agent.

I understood that *Cedar County* did not fit into a publishable category. It was not a work of history and was not quite a full-fledged memoir. I put the manuscript away and it stayed put away until the summer of 2002.

But, the business of publishing books has changed with the Internet and e-mail. Print-on-demand technology now allows anyone to write a book and get it into print with a minimum of expense and fuss. It may not sell but it's out there. With the help of technology and hugely-appreciated emotional and technical support from Toby Sonneman, *Cedar County* was revived and sent on its way.

◆   ◆   ◆

A lot of things happened between putting the manuscript away, I thought for good, in 1990, and looking at it again in a positive way in 2002. Living in Los Angeles with Carol didn't work out for me. I didn't fit in. I returned to Iowa City late in 1989, partly because my mother needed help with dad and her own health was failing. Another reason was I had no place I wanted to go. I helped mother put dad in a nursing home in early 1990, one of the hardest and saddest events of my life.

I lived with mother as she declined with congestive heart failure and lung troubles. I was asleep in the next room when she died in her bed sometime before sunrise on Sept. 23, 1990. One consolation was that I had helped her do what she had wanted, which was to die in her own home.

Dad was far gone with Alzheimer's by then but he did sense that mother had died. He often told me so. He hadn't lost all his personality either. One day toward the end of a nursing home visit, he was in his wheel chair but motioned me closer. He whispered in my ear, "Let's get out of here, get on the road to somewhere."

I sold the house early in 1991 and moved to Colorado to give it another try with Carol. This time we lived with her mother on a delightful small acreage in rim rock country south of Colorado Springs. It didn't work out. We fell out for good. We have lost touch. All I know is she went back to newspaper work and recently, at least, was the religion writer at a newspaper in Southern California.

After Colorado, I rented an apartment from Bob and Christine Gelms in an ancient general store building they owned in Springbrook, Iowa, not far from Bellevue. I stayed a while, doing some free lance magazine work and driving to Iowa City to see friends and visit dad at the nursing home.

In June, 1992, I moved to Cashmere, Washington, a pretty little town in the apple and pear country in the Wenatchee River Valley on the east slopes of the Cascades not far from the Columbia River. I wrote free lance articles for a tree fruit magazine and got by. In August, dad died a hard death at the nursing home. My brothers and I met in Iowa City for the memorial service. Bill was out of prison. He was working, coping, happy to be free.

Eventually, I met a good woman and we lived in Bellingham, Washington. I grew to dislike the town for its dampness of weather and affect. I returned to Cashmere and Toby and I have maintained a trans-mountain romance.

Brother Bill, a man I had grown close to, died of a cerebral hemorrhage in February, 2001, alone in his apartment in Salt Lake City. He was 49. Bill was cremated, and we could have sent his ashes to Iowa City to be buried next to our folks at Memory Gardens with a view of old U.S. 6 and a credit union. After some thought, Duane and I agreed Bill would have preferred a permanent address on the central California coast, an area he loved, and a more elegant address than he ever had in life.

We buried him on a sunny morning on a high headland north of Morro Bay, a golden coast, with a little bay on one side and open sea on the other. An unmarked grave on a headland, looking west, in what must be one of the most beautiful places on earth.

That about wraps up the changes between '88 and '02 except for a few postscripts. Christine and Bob Gelms were divorced. Christine, now Christine Baker, still runs the inn overlooking the Mississippi at Bellevue, Iowa. She spends most of her time in Muncie, Indiana, where she lives with her fourth husband, a professor of political science at Ball State University. Bob is a financial consultant in Dubuque. He remarried.

Ginny, the older of Christine and Bob's daughters, was in her second year at Northwestern University in Evanston, Ill. Bridget was a high school senior in Dubuque. When I talked to Christine by phone, I remarked on how fond I was of her girls back during the Victorian Summer. "Well, there's still a lot to be fond of where they are concerned," she said.

An e-mail from Bob added details. Ginny "rocketed" through high school and, at Northwestern, is interested in literature, linguistics and American Studies or all three, perhaps winding up with a doctorate. She is an accomplished pianist. Chicago, says her Chicago-native dad, is Ginny's "oyster and she is soaking the city up like a sponge."

Bridget is thinking about going to Ball State or the University of Northern Iowa. "She is a remarkably good actress," Bob said, and sometimes brings people "to tears with her performance." She is interested in film production, loves film noir and has expressed interest in social work. It looks like my instincts about these girls were on the mark.

Uncle Lester and Aunt Lorna, my congenial hosts in Lincoln, are gone and are buried in a little Catholic country cemetery north of Iowa City. I can't count the number of times I stopped overnight at their house on S. 36th St. during my unsettled and faintly demented period from '89 to '92 when I bounced back and forth every few months between Iowa, Colorado and the West Coast. In Lincoln, no matter how bad the weather, it was always the American Legion Club for dinner of catfish and a few Heinekens, and good talk with coffee around their kitchen table before I left in the morning. I doubt that I will ever stop in Lincoln again.

My old friend Quinn moved back to Iowa City years ago and lives in a downtown eighth-floor apartment with a nice view to the south. She'll retire before long and devote more time to writing her memoirs. As I looked at her small apartment recently, clean and orderly, I was reminded of something she told me years before. One morning drinking coffee at the Cottage near the campus, she said all she needed to be happy was her own room with a bed and a window, a private place to read and write.

Brother Duane and his partner Nancy left Fresno and live in Paso Robles, Calif., near the central coast, one of the most pleasant and livable towns in California. I see them frequently. My daughter, Nellie, stayed in Seattle, works for an architectural and interior design firm. She bought a house with a lovely backyard in the city's Ballard District.

The autumnal VW, my companion for 336,000 miles, retired from long distance and I traded it in on a new '98 red Honda Civic hatchback. The parting was more emotional than I would have guessed.

Over the years since leaving the *Seattle Post-Intelligencer* I occasionally produced something that went beyond hack work. Carol and I co-wrote a long piece about mountain lions for the *Los Angeles Times Magazine* and I've done some magazine work for Forbes Publications, including *American Heritage* magazine. My energy level flags at times but I'm not out of gas yet. I get royalty payments every three months for *Working on the Bomb*, the book about World War II plutonium production at Hanford, Washington.

My decision to leave a good reporting job in Seattle in 1988 at age 51 did not ruin me financially. When I was 55 I signed up for my semi-microscopic Hearst newspaper pension. At 62, I started Social Security, and at 65 signed up for Medicare. As Duane says, I have nothing more to look forward to.

Iowa City is still a good place, and I've visited a number of times over the years since I left Tipton. I don't like to stay away too long. Lots of changes, more people, landmarks diminishing in number, old roads replaced by new ones, some sadly familiar names in the graveyards. Still and all, it's my hometown and old friends are in residence.

◆   ◆   ◆

In November, 2002, I went back to Cedar County. My first stop was our old farm south of Tipton on what is now called "the Moscow

Road," named for the tiny town a few miles south of our place. I wanted to take what was probably a last walk on the road between our farm, now lacking a house and looking deserted, and the country school I attended in 1945. The country school had been torn down years ago.

I looked over the fence at the spot where the house had been, now a shallow depression in the ground, all that was left of what I recall was a handsome white square two-story house. The two big barns were gone, and so was the large shed near the house. No sign of the outdoor toilet or chicken house where dad had shot a chicken-eating owl one night. The hog houses were gone. So was the windmill. All that remained that I remembered were a decrepit corncrib, the falling-down garage where dad kept our Hudson Terraplane and the metal frame for the tractor gas tank.

The day, for November, was warm and sunny with a brisk north wind. I walked north toward the school site, no doubt looking like an older man whose car had broken down and was looking for a telephone. The brown countryside looked the same with well-tended corn and soybean fields, now all harvested. I remembered the farms. The Baker place across the road looked good. The road was paved, not gravel anymore, and traffic was fairly heavy and very fast compared with my lonely and quiet morning walks in 1945.

A large factory which makes hydraulic load-leveling equipment for recreational vehicles sprawls where the little country school building had been. The factory has been there for 35 years and just keeps getting bigger. A highway maintenance facility is a bit farther north. Interstate 80 rumbles past a couple of hundred yards away. The nearby Cove restaurant lives on. The distance from the farm was six-tenths of a mile and the walk took 10 minutes. I would have guessed from the perspective of my third grade mind that it was longer in distance and time.

This Cedar County visit was meant to be a brisk walk down Memory Lane, related both to my boyhood memories and those of my 1988 sojourn in Tipton. After my short walk, I drove north in a friend's

1988 Ford pickup with 88,088 miles on the clock. I was thrilled by the 88 coincidence. I headed for my old companion in solitude, the Rochester Cemetery across I-80.

The cemetery also looked good. New signs explained the cemetery was a fine example of the Oak Savanna Prairie of grasses and Bur oaks that once covered much of this part of Iowa. I walked around the spacious grassy place looking for old friends such as Mary "Granny" Sterrett, 1771–1870, and over on the far west end I found the simple stone that said: Grandmother Baker, died 1832 age 92. She must have been one of the first settlers to die in the newly-settled Iowa country. I stopped at a few of Christine's ancestors to say hello and tipped my cap at the many graves of Civil War veterans, including Richard Barnard, 24 years old, of Company G of the 35th Iowa Volunteers, who died months after the war ended, probably of battle wounds.

I drove north on Highway 38 and rolled into Tipton in the big '88 Ford and noticed right away the red-topped water tower looked a little off its feed. Fading paint, looking neglected. I found out later by reading the *Conservative* that the 71-year-old tower is not in great shape but should be safe until 2007.

Tipton had not changed a lot. The 2000 census said 3,155, which meant 100 more people than in 1988. Cedar County was home to 18,187, fewer than in 1980, and more than 1,000 fewer than in 1900. A couple of significant new businesses had moved in. One sold structural steel and the other, a unit of my old employer, The Hearst Corp., handled mailing for almost 500 magazines. The jail was new and the sheriff had a new office.

I hit the Maid-Rite for lunch. Still there and looking prosperous, with mostly large Chevy and Ford pickups parked next to the building. Prices seemed the same or almost. A Maid-Rite cost $2.15; two eggs, toast and coffee, $1.70; java, bottomless cup, 55 cents. It didn't look as if you could spend more than $4 for breakfast. New owners. Kay and Wally retired, although Wally works there on Mondays. Sadly for lonely guys like me, the Maid-Rite still doesn't open until 8 a.m., and is closed on Sundays. Same dependable topics at the counter. Sports and the weather. Customers were hefty and ate with customary gusto.

I swung past Judith Wacha's house. In '88 she wasn't sure she would stay in Tipton since she was there mostly because she had fallen in love with the big house, and not because Tipton seemed right for her. The house looked fine in pale yellow. I asked a man in the yard if Judith Wacha still lived there. "Nope. I bought this place six years ago and Judith Wacha moved back to Iowa City."

None of the priests and ministers I talked to were still in Tipton. Father Hines was dead and the others had moved on. The vets I spent time with, Krob and Esbeck, had retired. Sheriff Whitlatch had retired. At the Tipton Masonic Cemetery, I almost stumbled over the grave stone for Charlie Wright, the horse trainer I had interviewed, the talkative old fellow who was born in a log cabin in Kentucky. He died in 1993, a few days short of his 100th birthday.

One sign of life. The Hardacre movie house was still in business six days a week and showing up-to-date movies, seemingly more adult than the bubble-gum horrors Conn and I had endured.

I dropped in on Jerry Long, the county extension agent who succeeded my old landlord Ken Muller, who retired in about 1992. I was curious what had happened to the no till approach to farming, the technique that had fascinated me in '88. Long, who had come from Ohio, said no till had given way to minimum till, which was sort of halfway between the old way of plowing and disking and harrowing and the almost zero pre-planting preparation of no till. "You seldom see a plowed field anymore, but you do see fields that are lightly disked and harrowed before planting. The moldboard plow just isn't as popular as it was a few years ago."

Cedar County remains a place of family farms, he said, but acreage of the average farm has increased from 295 in 1987 to 338 in 1997. The routine remains corn and beans, hogs and cattle.

I found out that Kevin and Kerry Wright, the young farmer brothers I had talked to on the two occasions I went on rounds with vets

Krob and Esbeck, were still farming. But, they also had off-farm jobs in plumbing and carpentry. "They like that steady paycheck," their mother, Mary Wright, told me. The brothers, who liked raising hogs until hog prices got too low, are out of hogs and mostly rent land to farm from their dad, Alvin.

"Most young farmers have off-farm jobs now," Mrs. Wright said.

I talked to Stuart Clark, in 1988 the editor of the Tipton weekly paper. His father, Herb, was publisher. Stuart was one of the few people I spent much time with in Tipton when I lived there and I wondered then if he would make the newspaper his career as his father had done. He did, and apparently is doing well.

His dad died in 2000 in Ireland where he had a home on the Dingle Peninsula. Stuart, now 46, has taken over. In 2002 he bought two more nearby weeklies, in West Branch and West Liberty, and has owned the Hardacre Theater since 1991. The paper in Tipton has expanded into the "instant" passport photo business, "in stunning color, while you wait."

Entrepreneur Stuart was reasonably optimistic about Tipton. "Economically, Tipton is a relatively healthy county seat town," he said. I asked him why he was so busy with acquisitions. "I'm just trying to stay in the game," he replied.

One question had nagged at me over the years. What happened to Conner Meade, my "Irish degenerate" drinking buddy, the guy who couldn't wait to get out of Tipton. Stuart met Conn at Herb Clark's memorial service in Ireland. Conn was married, had three children and was an editor at an Irish newspaper. A fairly low-key outcome, I thought, for such a high-energy guy.

I saved a visit to Victorian House until the end of my Snotpit visit. I walked past the house, no longer called Victorian House, now a private residence lived in by Stuart and Paula Werling, an old Tipton family name. Both 46, he's an attorney and his wife runs a title abstract office. The house looked in good repair, in the middle of an ambitious many-colored paint renovation. White wicker furniture was on the porch, somewhat battered and the worse for wear. I assumed it was the same wicker the Gelms and I sat on during hot summer afternoons.

The evergreens Christine and I planted in the driveway on a long-ago summer afternoon were gone. I had naively thought they would be there long after me.

A plaque was attached to the wall to the left of the front door. It said: Reichert House, 1883, National Register of Historic Places. Victorian House had made it.

I went by twice and no one was home, except for an unfriendly dog in the backyard. The biggest change was the presence behind the house of an upscale three-door garage with matching driveway from East Fourth Street. I reached Paula Werling by telephone later and she told me the family (two children) had lived in the old house since 1996. She has become somewhat interested in antique furniture, partly because a number of antiques came with the house.

Naturally, I wondered if Ruby's ghost still lived in the old house, at least some of the time. Ms. Werling, without hesitation, said, "Yes, the ghost stories have continued, except the only person involved is my husband, Stuart. No one else has seen or heard anything."

Her husband, she said, has talked about the dining light going on and off for no reason, a door opening and shutting for no apparent reason. And he has heard footsteps when no one is present. She didn't seem disturbed or worried. Very matter of fact.

On the way out of town, at dusk, I stopped at the Tipton cemetery to say hello to Ruby, assuming she was there and not on haunting duty at the mansion. I found her modest gravestone in the Wingert family plot, and chatted about the good condition of her old house. I told Ruby the current residents were happy there and seemed to care for the place. I rambled on some more and then mentioned the northwest wind had become cold and blustery and it was time for me to be moving on.

0-595-26508-1

Printed in the United States
105893LV00004B/43/A